Inside SCIENCE

Infectious Disease Research

Other titles in the *Inside Science* series:

Biotech Research
Climate Change Research
Gene Therapy Research
Renewable Energy Research
Space Research
Stem Cell Research
Vaccine Research

Inside SCIENCE

Infectious Disease Research

Toney Allman

ReferencePoint Press®

San Diego, CA

© 2012 ReferencePoint Press, Inc.
Printed in the United States

For more information, contact:
ReferencePoint Press, Inc.
PO Box 27779
San Diego, CA 92198
www.ReferencePointPress.com

LIBRARY OF CONGRESS CATALOGING-IN-PUBLICATION DATA

Allman, Toney.
  Infectious disease research / by Toney Allman.
    p. cm. — (Inside science series)
  Includes bibliographical references and index.
  ISBN-13: 978-1-60152-177-4 (hardback)
  ISBN-10: 1-60152-177-4 (hardback)
  1. Communicable diseases—Juvenile literature. I. Title.
  RA643.A45 2012
  616.9—dc22
                                                        2011007745

Contents

Foreword

I n 2008, when the Yale Project on Climate Change and the George Mason University Center for Climate Change Communication asked Americans, "Do you think that global warming is happening?" 71 percent of those polled—a significant majority—answered "yes." When the poll was repeated in 2010, only 57 percent of respondents said they believed that global warming was happening. Other recent polls have reported a similar shift in public opinion about climate change.

Although respected scientists and scientific organizations worldwide warn that a buildup of greenhouse gases, mainly caused by human activities, is bringing about potentially dangerous and long-term changes in Earth's climate, it appears that doubt is growing among the general public. What happened to bring about this change in attitude over such a short period of time? Climate change skeptics claim that scientists have greatly overstated the degree and the dangers of global warming. Others argue that powerful special interests are minimizing the problem for political gain. Unlike experiments conducted under strictly controlled conditions in a lab or petri dish, scientific theories, facts, and findings on such a critical topic as climate change are often subject to personal, political, and media bias—whether for good or for ill.

At its core, however, scientific research is not about politics or 30-second sound bites. Scientific research is about questions and measurable observations. Science is the process of discovery and the means for developing a better understanding of ourselves and the world around us. Science strives for facts and conclusions unencumbered by bias, distortion, and political sensibilities. Although sometimes the methods and motivations are flawed, science attempts to develop a body of knowledge that can guide decision makers, enhance daily life, and lay a foundation to aid future generations.

The relevance and the implications of scientific research are profound, as members of the National Academy of Sciences point out in the 2009 edition of *On Being a Scientist: A Guide to Responsible Conduct in Research*:

Some scientific results directly affect the health and well-being of individuals, as in the case of clinical trials or toxicological studies. Science also is used by policy makers and voters to make informed decisions on such pressing issues as climate change, stem cell research, and the mitigation of natural hazards. . . . And even when scientific results have no immediate applications—as when research reveals new information about the universe or the fundamental constituents of matter—new knowledge speaks to our sense of wonder and paves the way for future advances.

The *Inside Science* series provides students with a sense of the painstaking work that goes into scientific research—whether its focus is microscopic cells cultured in a lab or planets far beyond the solar system. Each book in the series examines how scientists work and where that work leads them. Sometimes, the results are positive. Such was the case for Edwin McClure, a once-active high school senior diagnosed with multiple sclerosis, a degenerative disease that leads to difficulties with coordination, speech, and mobility. Thanks to stem cell therapy, in 2009 a healthier McClure strode across a stage to accept his diploma from Virginia Commonwealth University. In some cases, cutting-edge experimental treatments fail with tragic results. This is what occurred in 1999 when 18-year-old Jesse Gelsinger, born with a rare liver disease, died four days after undergoing a newly developed gene therapy technique. Such failures may temporarily halt research, as happened in the Gelsinger case, to allow for investigation and revision. In this and other instances, however, research resumes, often with renewed determination to find answers and solve problems.

Through clear and vivid narrative, carefully selected anecdotes, and direct quotations each book in the *Inside Science* series reinforces the role of scientific research in advancing knowledge and creating a better world. By developing an understanding of science, the responsibilities of the scientist, and how scientific research affects society, today's students will be better prepared for the critical challenges that await them. As members of the National Academy of Sciences state: "The values on which science is based—including honesty, fairness, collegiality, and openness—serve as guides to action in everyday life as well as in research. These values have helped produce a scientific enterprise of unparalleled usefulness, productivity, and creativity. So long as these values are honored, science—and the society it serves—will prosper."

Important Events in Infectious Disease Research

1890
Emil von Behring discovers the first antitoxins (antibodies against bacterial toxins) and develops vaccines against diphtheria and tetanus.

1870s
Robert Koch proves the germ theory of disease.

1867
Joseph Lister publishes his book about the importance of antiseptic surgical methods.

1670
Antonie van Leeuwenhoek refines the microscope and discovers blood cells and microorganisms.

1943
Selman A. Waksman discovers the antibiotic streptomycin.

| 1800 | 1850 | 1900 | 1950 |

1796
Edward Jenner develops the first vaccine; it protects against smallpox.

1928
Alexander Fleming discovers penicillin.

1885
Louis Pasteur develops the world's second vaccine, which prevents rabies.

1897
Ronald Ross proves that malaria is transmitted by mosquitoes.

1910
Paul Ehrlich discovers the "magic bullet" that selectively kills syphilis bacteria.

1954
Jonas Salk develops the first polio vaccine.

2006
The FDA approves Gardasil, the first vaccine for the prevention of a cancer; it prevents infection by the human papillomavirus.

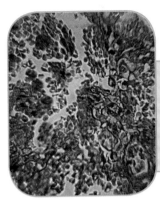

1987
AZT, the first antiretroviral drug for the treatment of AIDS, is introduced.

2011
Fidaxomicin, a new kind of antibiotic, is demonstrated to treat the intestinal infection *Clostridium difficile* better than existing antibiotics and without harming beneficial bacteria.

1980
The World Health Organization announces that smallpox has been eradicated.

| 1955 | 1970 | 1985 | 2000 | 2015 |

1983
Luc Montagnier and Françoise Barré-Sinoussi identify HIV, the virus that causes AIDS.

2010
The World Health Organization approves a new vaccine, MenAfriVac, for a type of meningitis that causes epidemics in sub-Saharan Africa.

1960
Methicillin, the first antibiotic to treat drug-resistant bacteria, is developed.

1999
The first medical reports are made of previously healthy young children dying of severe methicillin-resistant *Staphylococcus aureus* (MRSA) infections.

Devastating Diseases

After Haiti's destructive earthquake on January 12, 2010, infectious disease experts worried that outbreaks of infectious diseases would ensue. In October of that year, these fears became reality when the first reports of cholera emerged. The infection seemed to begin with a few people who drank water from the Artibonite River beside their village in Haiti, but it spread quickly from person to person and reached epidemic proportions throughout the country. People became ill with severe diarrhea and vomiting, and many died from dehydration, sometimes within hours of becoming ill.

Cholera is an infectious disease caused by a single-celled microscopic organism called a bacterium. The germ is shed in the feces of anyone infected by cholera. If any bit of feces contaminates the drinking water supply, anyone who drinks the water swallows cholera bacteria and is infected by the disease. The same thing can happen if people eat food that touched contaminated water or was touched by an infected person with bacteria on his or her fingers. As people become infected, they pass the disease along to others who pass it to others in an ever-widening geographical area. In a country such as Haiti where sewage structures and clean drinking water sources were devastated by an earthquake, the disease spreads rapidly. By December 26, 2010, cholera had infected close to 100,000 people in Haiti and was responsible for more than 3,300 deaths. The World Health Organization (WHO) estimated that as many as 650,000 people might be infected before the epidemic ran its course.

> **epidemic**
>
> A widespread outbreak of an infectious disease that affects many people at the same time.

Searching for Answers

As international medical teams struggled to treat the disease and prevent its spread, infectious disease researchers and scientists worked to understand how the cholera bacterium made its way to Haiti, whether a newly developed cholera vaccine would be valuable in preventing more cases, and what antibiotics would save the most lives. French infectious disease scientist and cholera specialist Renaud Piarroux studied the history and course of the outbreak and concluded that it began along the Artibonite River where a nearby United Nations (UN) camp of peacekeepers from Nepal was located. Cholera was previously unknown in Haiti, but it is common in Nepal. One of these peacekeepers, Piarroux theorized, apparently was carrying the cholera bacterium. The sewage from a leaky pipe at the UN camp, Piarroux suggested, somehow oozed into the Artibonite River, and then villagers along the river drank or bathed in the water. The Nepalese government and the UN angrily denied responsibility for the Haitian epidemic, but Piarroux said the outbreak could not be explained in any other way. On the basis of his research, he called for further investigation, better medical oversight of UN peacekeepers, and improved sanitation at UN camps.

Haitians suffering from cholera receive treatment in the aftermath of a devastating earthquake that struck Haiti in January 2010. As some researchers looked for the source of the infectious disease, others investigated the possible use of a new vaccine to halt its spread.

At the same time that Piarroux was conducting his research, other cholera specialists debated using a new cholera vaccine to prevent the spread of the disease. The newly developed vaccine can be administered in two oral doses, but supply was limited, and getting it to people throughout the country was deemed too difficult by some international health organizations. Paul Farmer, an infectious disease specialist at Harvard Medical School who works in Haiti, urged that the vaccine be rushed into production and used despite any difficulties. He also argued for the widespread use of antibiotics to treat people sick with cholera. He said that more lives would be saved if antibiotic treatments were used along with the fluid replacement that is currently the sole method of treating most sick people.

Driven to Stop the Devastation

Saving lives and easing suffering are the primary motivations behind the research of infectious disease experts such as Farmer and Piarroux. By identifying the sources of infectious diseases and developing treatments, they can prevent disease and death. Sunil Sazawal, a researcher and physician at the Johns Hopkins School of Public Health, says of his motives, "I would like to see my research prevent more deaths and morbidity than I could have prevented or treated as a physician."[1] Researchers provide the medical community with proven ways to improve treatment of infectious disease, new ways to prevent disease, and an increased understanding of the origins of infectious disease within a population.

According to the National Institute of Allergy and Infectious Diseases, a branch of the US government's National Institutes of Health, infectious diseases are the leading causes of death in many parts of the world. The organization Infection Research explains that disease-related death is not all that drives the research. Its website states,

> Above all, millions of people are disabled every year by infectious diseases. Measles, for example, can result in blindness, deafness or brain damage. Lymphatic filariasis, a parasitic worm disease also known as Elephantiasis, affects about 120 million people worldwide, and 40 million people are disabled and disfigured by it.

bacterium

A single-celled, living microorganism. The plural of *bacterium* is *bacteria*. Most bacteria are harmless or even helpful, but some may cause disease.

But the burden infectious diseases impose on humans goes far beyond the high death toll or the individual's fate. They keep children away from school and adults away from work. Costs for treatment are often unaffordable for patients and drive already poor families into ruin. The countrywide economic loss due to disease is immense, cementing poverty and underdevelopment in many regions of the world.[2]

This is the situation and the burden of global suffering that infectious disease researchers address and seek to change.

What Is Infectious Disease Research?

O n July 14, 2010, 10-year-old Liza Hollingsworth died. A few days earlier, the South Carolina girl had gone swimming in a lake where a killer lurked. It was an amoeba—a single-celled organism—that lives in mud at the bottom of warm, still, shallow ponds and lakes. The amoeba, scientifically named *Naegleria fowleri*, is a parasite, an organism that feeds on another living creature. Usually it feeds on lake bacteria, but if it infects people, the effects are swift and usually fatal. When water containing the amoebae is inhaled into the nose, these parasites travel through the olfactory nerve directly to the brain of the infected person. There, the amoebae feed on brain tissue. They release chemicals to dissolve the tissue, and as they feed, they basically leave holes in the brain.

The first symptoms of infection are nausea, headache, and fever, but the disease quickly progresses into brain inflammation, seizures, and then death. Only about 3 percent of people infected with *Naegleria fowleri* survive, usually because by the time it is accurately diagnosed, the infected person is too ill to be saved. Fortunately, infection is extremely rare. In 2010 only three other people besides Liza died of it in the United States. According to the Centers for Disease Control and Prevention (CDC), just 111 cases of the infection have been identified since 1962. Nevertheless, CDC infectious disease researchers are committed to finding out how to prevent the infection. One of these CDC scientists, Jonathan Yoder, said after Liza's death that he hopes that within two years CDC research will lead to sound advice about how to avoid infection.

Invading Organisms

Infectious disease research is the study of diseases caused by any organisms that infect the body and cause illness, whether the disease is a rare one such as *Naegleria fowleri* or a common one such as cholera. It involves identifying what causes the disease; determining effective treatments for the disease; developing educational guidelines for avoiding infection in a population, and learning to prevent the disease. It is research that touches every person on Earth because, at one time or another, everyone is threatened by infectious disease. Researchers are in a continual battle against the infectious agents that threaten humankind.

Organisms that cause infectious diseases are called pathogens. Parasites such as the amoeba *Naegleria fowleri* are pathogens, as are some bacteria, viruses, and fungi. Each kind of pathogen causes disease in a different way, but basically an infection is the colonization of the body by microorganisms that cause harm or disrupt body functions. When scientists refer to infection, they mean that a pathogen has gained access to the host's body and begun growing and reproducing. The pathogen invades body cells and tissues, and in the process of multiplying, it forms colonies of invaders that disrupt body functions by producing toxins (poisons) or damaging or killing cells. In this sense, all pathogens are parasites.

pathogens

Any microorganisms that cause disease.

Noninfectious diseases are not caused by pathogens. Heart disease and strokes, for example, are serious diseases that can cause disability and death, but they are not caused by infections. Diabetes, a disease in which the body is unable to control sugar levels in the blood, is not an infectious disease either. It is not caused by a pathogen invading the body but by a disruption in body functions. Most cancers also are not considered by experts to be infectious diseases (although some cancers can be triggered by infections). They cannot be transferred to other people. In other words, no one "catches" cancer, diabetes, or a heart attack from someone else.

Classifying Pathogens

Infectious pathogens, however, can be caught either from other people, animals, or directly from the environment (such as from organisms that live naturally in the water or soil). Infectious diseases are further classified as either communicable or noncommunicable, depending on how they are caught. Infectious diseases that are noncommunicable are caused by direct invasions of pathogens from the environment, but they are not readily spread from person to person. Tetanus, for example, is caused when tetanus bacteria living in soil enter an open wound. The invading bacteria cause severe sickness or death, but they remain inside the infected person and cannot spread to anyone else. Food poisoning is another example of a noncommunicable infection. It is caused by eating food contaminated by pathogens. These pathogens remain in the digestive system of the infected person and do not spread to other people.

A communicable disease is an infection that does spread from person to person. Infectious, communicable pathogens are transferable to other hosts (bodies)—theoretically infinitely. This transfer is what people usually refer to when they say a disease is "catching." Cholera is an example of a communicable disease; people catch it from one another. The bacteria in an infected person's feces spread to other people, perhaps when they swallow contaminated drinking water or care for a sick person and touch the diarrhea. The common cold is another example of a communicable disease. It can be transferred from person to person through the air or from surfaces that the infected person has touched. In the case of colds, the viruses that cause the infection spray into the air with coughs and sneezes or are transferred to the sick person's fingers and thus to surfaces that other people touch.

antibodies

Immune system factors that mark invaders for destruction.

Communicable diseases readily spread from person to person. A communicable disease that is easily transferred to other people is called a contagious disease. Influenza and the common cold, for example, are contagious diseases. Contagious diseases can lead to epidemics, such as the cholera epidemic in Haiti. Throughout human history, infectious disease researchers have worried most about contagious diseases because such diseases have caused widespread suffering and death. The effort to understand and control these infectious diseases, however, did not succeed for centuries. The problem was that researchers could not see the pathogens nor understand what they did.

Mysterious Diseases of Civilization

Epidemiologists—researchers who specialize in the study of epidemics and disease transmission—believe that epidemics of diseases began when people started to live together in large groups and to establish cities. Civilization brought many advantages, but, says science writer Jessica Snyder Sachs, "the tradeoff [was] crowding and water contamination."[3] Cities were a perfect environment for the spread of pathogens. Records of epidemics exist for the ancient city of Sumer from 4,000 years ago. Such records also exist for Egypt, India, and China from as early as 3700 BC.

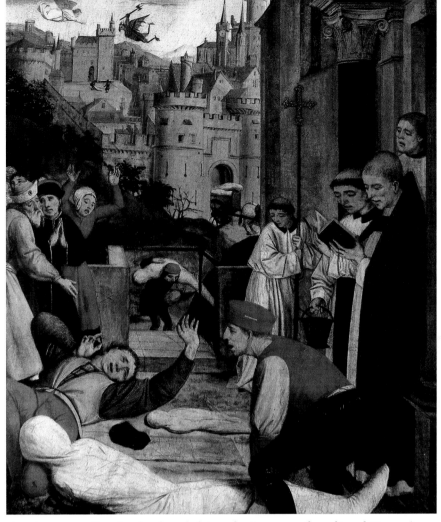

A priest prays for the dead and dying during one of medieval Europe's periodic bouts with bubonic plague, known at the time as the Black Death. Medieval doctors had no real understanding of infectious diseases so they blamed outbreaks on bad air and other unseen causes.

Early doctors and healers understood, even then, that the diseases were passed from person to person, but they had no idea why or how. By the fourteenth century, when the Black Death killed perhaps half of Europe's population, doctors blamed epidemics on bad air, or miasmas, and attempted in primitive ways to guard against contagion. For many doctors of the time this meant fleeing the areas where the plague was rampant, but for others it meant wearing protective face masks to prevent the doctor from breathing the supposed bad air during visits to sick patients. Some doctors even smeared their coats with animal fat in hope of trapping any airborne poisons.

The First Use of Penicillin

Albert Alexander, a 43-year-old London policeman, was the first human volunteer to try penicillin. Researchers Howard Florey, Ernst Chain, and Norman Heatley of Oxford University had experimented with the penicillin molds discovered by Alexander Fleming for years. They grew it in dishes and worked to purify it and make a penicillin factory in their laboratory. In tests with their penicillin in mice, they proved that it could stop streptococcus infections. The work to grow and purify the drug was slow, and they got little usable medicine, but on February 21, 1941, they tried to treat Alexander with the penicillin they did have.

He had scratched the side of his mouth while pruning roses in his garden and developed a terrible infection at the site of the wound. He had huge open sores and abscesses on his face and eyes that had spread to his lungs. He had already lost one eye and was dying. The scientists began treating Alexander by injecting him with penicillin. The results were remarkable. After five days, his fever disappeared, he had an appetite, and the infection on his face was nearly gone. But then their supply of penicillin was used up. The infection returned, and Alexander died several days later. Nevertheless, Alexander had shown that penicillin could conquer infection, and later, with larger quantities of their new drug, the researchers saved the lives of other patients.

Today, researchers believe that the Black Death was really bubonic plague, a bacterial disease carried by the fleas that infested city rats and then jumped on people. Epidemics of bubonic plague periodically ravaged areas of Europe and Asia for centuries, but no one suspected rats or their fleas to be the cause, much less unseen germs.

Discovering the Enemy

True understanding of infectious disease did not begin until the invention of the microscope and the experiments of Antonie van Leeuwenhoek in the Netherlands. In 1670, after learning about the microscope from other early scientists, Leeuwenhoek made his own microscope and examined his own saliva. In a letter at the time, he marveled, "I then most always saw, with great wonder, that in the said matter [his saliva] there were many very little living animalcules, very prettily a-moving."[4] He had discovered microbes, but he had no idea that such tiny creatures could harm humans. A century later, a few doctors did begin to suggest that microbes might cause disease, but most doctors rejected the idea even into the nineteenth century.

One medical expert of the nineteenth century, Jacob Henle, did believe, but he knew that scientific proof was necessary. He lectured his students that microbes could not be proved to cause disease unless they were always found in material (such as saliva, blood, or pus) from a sick person. In addition, he said, these microscopic animalcules would have to be isolated in the laboratory, given to other people or animals in pure form, and then be shown to cause sickness. Only then would the medical world believe that microbes were the cause of disease.

One of Henle's students in Germany, Robert Koch, did exactly as his professor suggested. In 1876 he began using his microscope to study the bacteria in the blood of animals with anthrax and tuberculosis. Both diseases infect people as well as animals. Koch found that he could see the bacteria when he stained them with dyes. He figured out how to isolate the stained bacteria from infected blood and then grow the bacteria in the laboratory. Next he injected the bacteria into healthy mice in his laboratory and watched them sicken and die. When he injected the mice with fluids and even blood that contained no bacteria, the

> ### *Staphylococcus*
>
> A large genus of bacteria that are spherical in shape and can cause many diseases and infections.

mice remained healthy. He had proved scientifically that microbes were the cause of diseases. He also showed that particular bacteria cause particular diseases. In other words, the bacterium named *Bacillus anthracis* caused anthrax but never tuberculosis.

More Breakthroughs

Around the same time that Koch was performing his research in Germany, medical researchers elsewhere worked to find ways to attack disease-causing microbes and destroy them. English doctor Joseph Lister proved that bathing surgical instruments, bandages, and even patients' wounds with carbolic acid stopped infections by killing microbes. French scientist Louis Pasteur proved with laboratory experiments that microbes do not grow spontaneously in the air or in bodies. His experiments demonstrated that germs are transferred from one body to another. Pasteur learned that heat kills microbes and discovered that heating, or "pasteurizing," milk killed the tuberculosis bacteria that lurked in diseased cows' milk and infected the people who drank it. His research showed that infections came from an identifiable source and were contagious and that it was possible to stop or prevent contagion by killing microbes.

Louis Pasteur, portrayed in his lab, conducted experiments on rabid dogs. This work led to a vaccine for rabies and contributed to an understanding of immune response and infection in humans and animals.

Pasteur also discovered another way to fight infectious pathogens. He developed some of the world's earliest vaccines. Vaccines prevent disease by using the body's natural immune system. The immune system is the body's complex way of defending itself from outside invasions of microbes. Immune system defenses include antibodies that grab onto invading organisms and mark them for destruction by immune system killer cells. The body's immune system prevents invasions by most pathogens, but serious infections can overwhelm the immune system defenders before they have the chance to mount a full defense. Vaccines, which contain weakened or killed invader microbes, are injected into the bloodstream where the immune system learns to make antibodies against them. Once the antibodies have been activated in this way, they are ready to fight any real invasion in the future, and they prevent the vaccinated individual from getting sick. The invading microbes are destroyed so quickly that they can do no harm. In 1881 Pasteur developed a vaccine against anthrax, a disease of cattle. In 1885 he developed a vaccine for people against rabies, an almost always fatal disease.

The period of history between 1857 and 1914 is called the Golden Age of Microbiology. It began with the research of Koch and Pasteur and continued with microbiologists and medical researchers determined to understand and fight infectious microbes. The infectious disease researchers of this time demonstrated that the germ theory of disease was accurate, identified many of the specific organisms that caused different diseases, and began the search for the agents that might kill or prevent the invasion of infectious microorganisms. With each new discovery, excited researchers were emboldened to search for the way to fight microbes and win the battle against infectious disease.

The First Microbe Killers

Paul Ehrlich, who began his career as a researcher in Koch's Institute for Infectious Diseases in Germany in the late 1870s, originated the idea of "magic bullets" to fight microbes. He knew that the dyes used by Koch had stained bacterial cells because the cells absorbed the dye even though human and animal cells did not. Bacterial cells absorbed substances that other cells could resist. Ehrlich wondered if he could find a dye or chemical that when absorbed would poison the bacterial cell without harming the other cells. Such dyes, or chemicals, would be magic bullets that killed only bacteria. Ehrlich explained, "Here we may speak of 'magic bullets' which aim exclusively at the dangerous intruding [parasitic] strangers to the organism, but do not touch the organism itself and its cells."[5]

In 1905 Ehrlich embarked on a study to find the dye that could attack and kill the bacteria that cause syphilis. During his time, this sexually transmitted disease existed in epidemic proportions throughout much of the world. It caused sores and rashes on the entire body and, in its later stages, caused brain damage, blindness, heart disease, and death. Each year thousands of people were disabled or killed by the disease. Using animals in his laboratory, Ehrlich tested 605 different chemical compounds until he found the one, on June 8, 1909, that he called compound 606; it was his magic bullet against the bacteria that cause syphilis.

Ehrlich's discovery was the world's first artificial antibiotic drug, but it was not the last. His compound 606 led to the discovery of sulfa drugs, which like Ehrlich's antibiotic are derived from dyes. These drugs could kill some microbes but not all. Then, in 1928 Alexander Fleming discovered that a mold called *Penicillium glaucum* selectively killed *Staphylococcus* bacteria. *Staphylococcus*, or staph, for short, is a large genus of bacteria that can cause infections in many areas of the body. In 1940 the first true antibiotic—penicillin—was developed from the chemicals in the *Penicillium glaucum* mold that killed bacteria. Penicillin is called a true antibiotic because it is a microbe-killing drug derived from another microbe. It is effective against other bacteria, such as *Streptococcus*, too.

mutations

Permanent changes in genetic material that alter coded information and heredity.

Miracle Antibiotics?

During the 1930s researchers turned their attention to ordinary soil and the microbe-killing microbes, such as bacteria, that live in dirt. More microbes live in a single gram of soil than the number of people who live on Earth. They get their food by secreting chemicals that decompose organic matter. They protect themselves by secreting other chemicals that kill other kinds of microbes that intrude into their space. For microbiologists and infectious disease researchers, discovery of these microbes led to a golden age of antibiotic development between 1950 and 1960. The microbe-killing chemicals in bacteria led to the discovery of antibiotics such as streptomycin, which could kill tuberculosis bacteria; tetracycline, a broad-spectrum

Reservoirs

For pathogens, a reservoir is the place where they survive. It can be people, animals, water, soil, or any substance in which the pathogen naturally lives and multiplies. With some diseases, such as measles, humans are the only reservoir. The measles virus cannot infect any other organisms. For many other diseases, however, the reservoir is the place where a pathogen safely hides when no humans are infected. Sometimes, the reservoir of a pathogen is well known to scientists, but at other times, it is a mystery.

In 2001, for example, a kind of influenza, called type A influenza, was infecting people in Hong Kong. Researchers did not know what caused the outbreak but finally were able to trace the infection to chickens. People in contact with farm chickens were catching the flu and spreading it to others. Rabies is another example of a pathogen for which animals are the reservoir. Wild deer are the reservoir for Lyme disease, which is then spread to humans by ticks that feed on the deer and then bite humans. The reservoir for the bacterium that causes tetanus is the soil, while the reservoir for the lung infection Legionnaires' disease is water. Identification of the reservoir is often critical when researchers are trying to fight a disease outbreak. For example, Hong Kong government officials stopped the spread of type A influenza by slaughtering the infected poultry. Legionnaires' disease, on the other hand, is prevented by careful cleaning and disinfecting of water systems to which people are exposed.

antibiotic that kills many kinds of infectious bacteria; and cephalosporin, which can kill *Streptococcus* bacteria. Antibiotics seemed to be miracle drugs. They could not kill viruses or fungi, but they seemed to infectious disease researchers to be the answer to all infectious bacteria.

Many researchers believed it was only a matter of time before all infectious diseases were conquered. In 1962 the Nobel Prize–winning Australian medical researcher Macfarlane Burnet wrote that "at times one feels that to write about infectious disease is almost to write of something that has passed into history."[6]

Burnet was wrong. Today, pathogens are far from conquered. Medical researcher F. Gonzalez-Crussi calls pathogens "overwhelmingly powerful." He says, "Bacteria, viruses, and fungi have a history of resiliency and survival that ought to humble the omnipresent pride of our species, if we so much as fleetingly consider the facts. Bacteria were present billions of years before there was any intimation [hint] of the human race, and it is a safe wager that they will be around long after the last trace of mankind has vanished."[7]

How They Do It

Microbes are so successful because they are capable of quickly adapting to their environments. When they infect a host, they are genetically programmed to survive and thrive there. All living things carry genetic instructions inside their cells. These instructions are the blueprint for how that organism grows, develops, functions, and reproduces. Microbes can adapt to a change in the environment, such as a killing medicine, because their genetic instructions can rapidly evolve and change. Both bacteria and viruses evolve and resist efforts to kill and control them as they multiply inside a host.

Viruses are not exactly living, but they are packages of genetic instructions in the form of deoxyribonucleic acid (DNA) or ribonucleic acid (RNA). The virus's genetic instructions allow it to slip inside a host's cell and inject its genetic instructions into the host's DNA. These instructions take over the host cell and direct it to manufacture more viruses. The viruses explode out of the cell, killing it, and go on to infect more cells. If the viruses are ones that cause colds, for example, they infect human respiratory cells. Bacteria are much more complex. A typical bacterium is a single cell surrounded by a protective capsule or shell; inside its shell, the bacterium's genetic material is arranged as a long strand of DNA. Bacteria invade host organisms and act as parasites inside the host's body. They multiply by cell division and often secrete toxins as they multiply.

resistance

The ability of a microorganism to survive a toxic agent, such as an antibiotic medication, because of mutation.

Both bacteria and viruses quickly multiply, or replicate themselves, inside human bodies. When they do, their genetic instructions are copied, and sometimes mistakes, somewhat like typographical errors, occur in the copying processes. These mistakes, called mutations, are changes in the genetic code of the pathogens. Some of these changes are beneficial to the

How Viruses Infect the Body

Viruses, which enter the body through breaks, scratches, or imperceptible tears in the skin, are microscopic fragments of nucleic acid that are enclosed in protein shells. Unlike cells and bacteria, viruses cannot reproduce on their own; instead, they must invade living "host" cells and use the cells as factories where they produce more viral material, and in this way they lead to various types of infection. This illustration shows the progression.

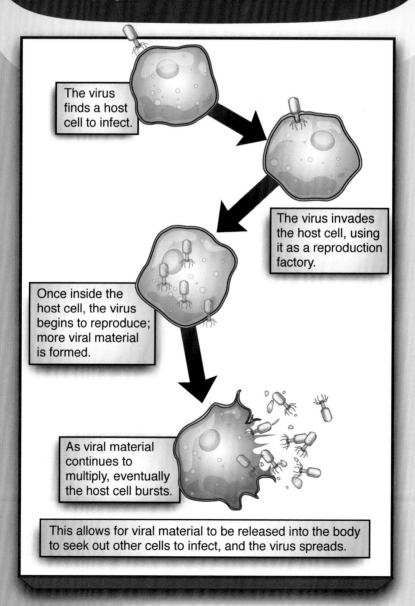

The virus finds a host cell to infect.

The virus invades the host cell, using it as a reproduction factory.

Once inside the host cell, the virus begins to reproduce; more viral material is formed.

As viral material continues to multiply, eventually the host cell bursts.

This allows for viral material to be released into the body to seek out other cells to infect, and the virus spreads.

Source: Craig Freudenrich, "How Viruses Work," How Stuff Works, 2000. http://health.howstuffworks.com.

pathogens. The host's immune system may no longer be able to fight off the pathogen because it has so many variations. Mutations may make a vaccine ineffective or impossible to develop. They may make a bacterial pathogen able to survive a microbe-killing antibiotic. In the war against infectious disease, the pathogens that evolve and develop into new strains win.

Continual Research Required

Microbiologist Julian Davies says that a "steady evolution" of bacteria has been happening since antibiotics were first discovered. He says, "Within two to three years after the introduction of a new antibiotic treatment, resistance usually develops."[8] Resistance is the ability of a pathogen to survive and tolerate, or resist, a specific antibiotic. Almost all infectious bacteria today are resistant to one or more antibiotics. Thus, bacterial diseases once thought conquered are reemerging as threats to people.

Viruses have also proven difficult to conquer. Because they mutate so easily, they can emerge as new diseases by evolving and developing the ability to infect new hosts, such as moving from birds to humans, as bird flu has done. They can resist the efforts of researchers to find treatments just because their genetic material is so variable that no one drug or vaccine can attack all the different strains. Parasites usually have such complex life cycles—being dependent on animal hosts and then invading human hosts—that eradicating them seems beyond medical possibility, even when an individual can be treated.

Sometimes humankind seems to be in a losing battle with infectious microbes, but infectious disease researchers continue to fight. With constant vigilance, they strive to identify, treat, and prevent infectious diseases of all types.

Identification and Diagnosis Research

Every pathogen that threatens people is different, and each requires a specific treatment or medical intervention. For example, what kills one bacterium may not harm another. A vaccine that triggers antibody production for one virus has no effect on antibody production for another kind. A medicine that kills the eggs of one parasite may not kill others. Therefore, accurate diagnosis—identifying which pathogen has infected a person—is extremely important. Identification of pathogens and the ability to readily diagnose diseases are major goals of infectious disease research.

The Right Test for Correct Diagnosis

Today, scientists have identified thousands of pathogens that infect people, but that does not always mean that diseases are easy for doctors to diagnose. Even when the pathogen is known to medicine, testing for it in a particular individual can be a problem. In 1990, for instance, Danielle Jordan (real name withheld for her privacy) faced dangerous brain surgery if her infection was not correctly diagnosed. One day, the California woman suddenly began slurring her words. She had muscle spasms on the right side of her face and numbness in her right hand. Jordan's doctor ordered a CT (computed tomography) scan of her brain. The complex X-rays revealed a pea-sized lesion in her brain that looked like a tumor. To be sure, the doctor arranged for Jordan to have an MRI (magnetic resonance imaging) study done. The detailed pictures from this test suggested a malignant brain tumor, and Jordan was referred to a brain surgeon. Even with surgery, she remembers, "he told me I had a very bad brain tumor and that I had only a 50 percent chance of being alive in three years."[9]

Fortunately, Jordan got a second opinion before her brain surgery was performed. This doctor looked at her test results and doubted the diagnosis. He thought the lesion looked like cysticercosis: the medical name for a parasitic tapeworm larva in her brain. He referred Jordan to infectious disease specialist Pamela Nagami for diagnosis and treatment. Tapeworms are common parasites. A tapeworm up to 60 feet long can live inside a person's intestines. There, it produces eggs that are shed in the person's feces. These eggs may end up on the person's hands if he or she does not wash carefully after bathroom use. Under such unsanitary conditions, those eggs—sometimes many of them—may contaminate anything the person touches, such as food. Anyone who eats the food and swallows the eggs is infected. As in Jordan's case, the eggs can travel throughout the body and often end up lodged in the brain where they hatch into larvae—little worms called cysticerci. This, Nagami believed, was what had happened to Jordan. On a vacation in Mexico she ate a salad at a restaurant. Someone working at the restaurant probably had a tapeworm. Tapeworm eggs on the person's hands were transferred to the salad served to Jordan.

Nagami, however, did not want to treat Jordan for the wrong disease. Diagnosis of Jordan's cysticercosis depended on a blood test that had just been developed by the CDC. Instead of taking months, as older tests did, this new test could analyze blood in days. Nagami sent a sample of Jordan's blood to the Parasitic Diseases Branch of the CDC. Scientists there were not sure that their new test for cysticercosis was sensitive enough to identify antibodies in blood for just one cyst in the brain, but the test was fast and easy. The scientists tested the blood sample, and it came back positive for cysticercosis. Nagami says, "They were delighted that their new test had registered a positive in a patient with just one worm."[10] Treatment was now simple; the right medicine killed the worm and cured Jordan. In addition, Jordan's blood test was evidence for the CDC that their new test was effective.

lesion

An abnormal change in the structure of an organ or tissue caused by disease or injury.

A New Diagnostic Test for an Old Disease

Infectious disease researchers know that tests that decrease diagnosis time can save lives. That was the goal of David Alland, the chief of the infectious diseases division of the University of Medicine and Dentistry of New Jersey. He developed a new way to diagnose tuberculosis (TB). TB is caused by the bacterium *Mycobacterium tuberculosis*. Approximately one-third of the world's people are infected by the bacterium, mostly in underdeveloped countries, and of those people about 10 percent develop

Tapeworms attach to the intestinal walls of their host by means of hooks (top) and suckers, four of which are visible in this false-color light micrograph. Eggs from the mature tapeworm are shed in a person's feces.

active TB. Active TB most often attacks and eats holes in the victim's lungs. In the active stage, a TB victim is contagious and spreads the disease to others whenever he or she coughs or even breathes the bacteria into the air. Approximately 1.6 million people die of TB each year. To make matters worse, *Mycobacterium tuberculosis* has developed many drug-resistant forms that are difficult to treat.

The traditional test for TB is more than 100 years old and is called a sputum test; it is a test of the saliva. Doctors take a sample of a patient's saliva and send it to a medical laboratory. Laboratory technicians place the specimen on a petri dish and then grow a culture. This means that the saliva is added to a mixture of nutrients on which bacteria can feed, divide, and grow into a colony. Finally, the culture can be examined under a

The Nobel Laureate

Françoise Barré-Sinoussi was born in Paris, France, in 1947. She did not come from a family that was particularly interested in science or research, but from childhood, she was always fascinated by biology and learning about living things. When she went to college, she studied science and eventually got her doctorate in virology, the science of viruses. She had a special interest in retroviruses.

She began working at the Institut Pasteur laboratories in Paris, and it was there, as a young researcher in 1982, that she became interested in the mystery pathogen that was causing the new disease called AIDS. When the laboratory received a sample from a person with AIDS in January 1983, Barré-Sinoussi went to work on the experiments that first proved AIDS was caused by a retrovirus that would later be identified as HIV.

Since that time, Barré-Sinoussi has assisted other AIDS researchers and has worked with international humanitarian organizations that try to reduce the transmission of HIV. Being awarded the Nobel Prize in Physiology or Medicine, which she received in 2008, did not halt her work. She continues her AIDS research and works to educate and inspire future scientists. She says, "There is always hope in life because there is always hope in science."

Quoted in Neda Afsarmanesh, "Under the Lens: Françoise Barré-Sinoussi: The 35th Woman Nobel Laureate," Under the Microscope, October 19, 2008. www.underthemicroscope.com.

microscope for the presence of TB bacteria. The whole process can take as long as three months, and during that waiting time, the patient can infect other people, get worse, or even die.

But in 2010 Alland changed all that. He used DNA technology—the same kind that DNA labs use to identify criminals or that genetic labs use to diagnose hereditary diseases—to develop a test for TB bacteria. Bacteria are as unique as people in regard to their DNA. Alland developed a computerlike machine to test for the unique DNA of *Mycobacterium tuberculosis*. The machine can examine sputum samples and identify the presence of TB bacteria. Saliva from a patient is put inside a little cup and then inserted into the machine. Through a complex series of steps, the machine analyzes the DNA and then generates a printout of the results. Alland explains, "The test will say whether TB is there or not, and whether the TB is drug-resistant. Overall, the test picks up 98 percent of all TB. . . . It picks up strains the microscope misses."[11] The test can identify drug-resistant TB strains, because their DNA is slightly different from the DNA of regular TB, and it can complete its analysis in 100 minutes. Anyone using the test quickly knows whether an individual has TB and what kind of medicine will work best to cure it.

Around the world, infectious disease researchers hailed Alland's new TB test. On December 8, 2010, the World Health Organization (WHO) endorsed use of the new machine for the world's most at-risk people in Asia and Africa. The director of WHO's Stop TB Department, Mario Raviglione, says, "This new test represents a major milestone for global TB diagnosis and care. It also represents new hope for the millions of people who are at the highest risk of TB and drug-resistant disease."[12] Fred Tenover, a director at Cepheid, the genetics company that helped Alland's team develop his technology, says, "I'm sure Koch and Pasteur would not only be delighted with the technological advance, they would probably say, 'It's about time.'"[13]

Rapid Identification Needed

Other infectious disease researchers are working on the diagnosis of a serious parasitic disease called visceral leishmaniasis (VL). The disease parasite lives in sandflies in Africa, India, Southeast Asia, and Latin America. It is transmitted to people when they are bitten by infected sandflies. The parasite enters the victim's body and then migrates to bone marrow and organs such as the liver and spleen. People suffer with fever, anemia, weight loss, and organ damage. VL is almost always fatal when it is not treated. Each year about 500,000 people are infected with VL. According to the nonprofit Infectious Disease Research Institute (IDRI) of Seattle, Washington, an estimated 50,000 people die—most of them children—because the disease is not diagnosed soon enough for treatment. Diagnosis often depends on surgically removing a piece of infected organ and examining it under a microscope. Besides being a painful procedure, it is usually not available in poor, underdeveloped areas.

larva

The newly hatched, wormlike form of an organism (e.g., insect or parasite) that has not yet changed into the adult form. Plural is *larvae*.

Steven Reed of IDRI and his research partner, Yasuyuki Goto, are working to develop a rapid diagnostic test for VL. Their goal is to be able to find evidence of leishmaniasis infection in a single drop of a sick person's blood. In 1994 Reed and a scientific team were able to identify some antibodies made by the immune system in response to VL and test for them successfully. Their test involved combining a protein called K39 with a blood sample. Healthy people have no antibody response to K39, but blood infected with VL does react to K39. The test is fast and simple to perform. In trials throughout the 1990s, the researchers found that the test works for infected people in India, Brazil, Bangladesh, and Nepal where leishmaniasis is caused by one particular species of parasite. Where other parasite species are involved, such as in Africa, the test does not work.

Today, Reed and Goto are working to identify all the substances in leishmaniasis parasites that provoke the immune system to make antibodies. Substances on the surface of pathogens that cause an antibody response are called antigens. Reed and Goto are trying to identify the important antigens on leishmaniasis parasites wherever in the world they may occur. Then they hope to combine K39 with laboratory proteins that mimic these antigens. If they succeed, leishmaniasis antibodies in a drop of blood would react to such a substance. And that would mean a rapid, easy diagnosis of VL anywhere in the world.

Identification of an Unknown Pathogen

Researchers such as Reed and Goto, who are trying to develop tests for known pathogens, have a big advantage: They know what the pathogen is, how it infects people, and even its genetic makeup. When a new disease appears, however, identification is much more difficult. This was the case in 1981 when the CDC received its first reports of a serious new disease. Five men in three different hospitals in Los Angeles were suffering from a rare kind of pneumonia that infects only people who have extremely weak immune systems. The men had other unusual diseases, too, and no one knew why. CDC scientists speculated that a contagious pathogen might be at work, and by 1982 they determined that it was a blood-born infectious disease, appearing in many countries around the world. The CDC named the unknown disease "acquired immune deficiency syndrome," or AIDS. Somehow, a pathogen was destroying people's immune systems so that their bodies could not fight off unusual invaders.

In 1983 French researchers Luc Montagnier and Françoise Barré-Sinoussi of the Pasteur Institute set out to find the pathogen that causes AIDS. Barré-Sinoussi suspected that it was a retrovirus, although, at that time, scientists knew of only two retroviruses. A retrovirus is a virus that consists of a package of RNA rather than DNA for its coding instructions. RNA is a kind of decoded DNA that mimics the messages of the living cells that the virus infects. Barré-Sinoussi acquired the lymph node of a young person who had died of AIDS. She analyzed the lymph node to find the protein, an enzyme, used by retroviruses to cause chemical reactions that allow them to take over the functions of a host's cell. Barré-Sinoussi did find an enzyme, but it was not an enzyme from any known retrovirus. After many tests, Montagnier identified the new retrovirus as the cause of AIDS. Today, it is known as the human immunodeficiency virus (HIV). Montagnier and Barré-Sinoussi won the 2008 Nobel Prize in Physiology or Medicine for their discovery. By identifying HIV, they made it possible for other researchers to develop diagnostic tests for HIV and then to develop treatments for it.

> **culture**
>
> Laboratory cultivation of microorganisms in a nutrient substance in which they feed and reproduce.

Diagnosing AIDS

Researchers with the pharmaceutical company Abbott Laboratories developed the first diagnostic test for AIDS. It identified antibodies to HIV in the blood of an infected person. This test is still used today, but rapid HIV testing is also available. Rapid HIV tests work both with a drop of blood or a swab of the inside of the mouth. With one kind of test, samples are put on a small paddle that is infused with antigens to HIV. If any HIV antibodies are in the sample, a strip on the paddle reacts and turns red after 20 minutes. These tests are easy to use and inexpensive but not always accurate. Sometimes the rapid tests give false positive results; this means that the strip turns red even though the sample does not have HIV.

In New York City, researchers at the Department of Health and Mental Hygiene did a study of all rapid testing between 2005 and 2008. They determined that out of 166,058 tests during that time, 44 were

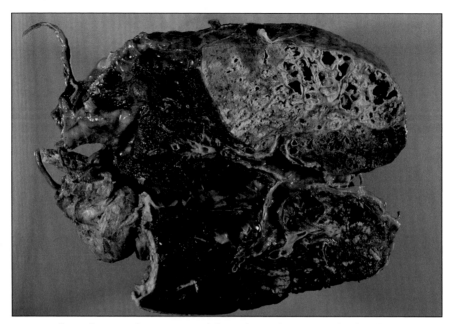

Pictured are human lungs scarred by tuberculosis. Newly developed DNA testing technology can confirm the presence of tuberculosis in just under two hours—a significant improvement on previous methods that could take up to three months.

false positives. The number is small, but the New York Department of Health and Mental Hygiene decided to stop using the rapid HIV tests in 2008. Other health departments in the United States still use the tests to screen people but always check positive results with the original blood test. In some parts of Africa, however, the rapid tests may be used alone because of cost issues. In 2009 Kenyan researchers Peter Cherutich and Omu Anzala studied the rapid test results of 6,255 people and found 131 testing errors. The scientists concluded that thousands of people across Kenya and neighboring Uganda might be told they have AIDS when they do not. Researchers, in hope of making rapid testing more accurate, are still trying to understand why some people have false positive results.

Infectious disease researchers have a lot to learn about identifying HIV, not because diagnosing an individual is difficult but because HIV mutates very easily and has developed different strains. This means that the antigens that antibodies latch onto are different across the different strains. HIV-1 is the most prevalent in Western countries, but HIV-2 is most common in Africa. Each of these HIV types can exist in hundreds of variations. In 2007, for example, a group of New York researchers discovered that some people with HIV were infected with retroviruses that had drug-resistant mutations. Effective AIDS treatment depends on identifying such dangerous strains, so researchers continue to try to monitor these mutations around the world.

The Threat of a Mutated Virus

Sometimes viral mutations mean that a virus that infects only animals can suddenly infect humans, often with deadly results. Many researchers believe that this is how AIDS became a human disease. It mutated and jumped from being able to infect monkeys to invading people. Such new viral diseases can strike without warning, and infectious disease researchers must be able to recognize their appearance quickly if they are to prevent epidemics and save lives. This is what WHO infectious disease specialist Carlo Urbani did in 2003. On February 28 a hospital in Hanoi, Vietnam, asked WHO for help. The hospital doctors thought they had a patient with a serious kind of influenza, and they wanted help identifying it. Urbani went to the hospital to evaluate the situation. Almost immediately he determined that the man, Johnny Chen, did not have flu. He had a serious pneumonia of unknown cause.

Urbani worked at the hospital, gathering information about symptoms and determining with blood samples that the pneumonia was not caused by any known pathogen. Already, several hospital workers were developing symptoms of the disease, so Urbani knew that it was contagious. He set up isolation procedures at the hospital. Infected patients were separated from other patients and visitors; the staff wore masks, gloves, and gowns and sterilized anything that contacted infected people. Urbani also collected blood samples from the infected patients and sent them to several laboratories, asking for identification help. He warned WHO that this disease, which he labeled severe acute respiratory syndrome (SARS), threatened to spread into a terrible epidemic.

antigens

Any substances that provoke an immune system response and the production of antibodies.

Because of his quick reaction, a global SARS epidemic was averted. Laboratory researchers identified the virus in his samples as a mutated virus that had probably jumped from animals to people in China. Doctors in China were reporting the deaths of patients with a strange "flu." Researchers later learned that Chen had flown to Hanoi from China just a

Testing the Waters for Humans' Sake

Researchers do not always concentrate on diagnosing infections in humans. Preventing diseases by identifying threatening pathogens in the environment is also a priority. In 2011 scientists at the US Department of Agriculture (USDA) developed a new method of testing waterways, such as ponds and lakes, for *Escherichia coli* and *Salmonella* bacteria, which often sicken people when they are exposed to just a few of the pathogens. Identifying these pathogens in food is not difficult, but in water they can often escape detection.

The USDA scientists developed a special filter in which to put water samples, used a centrifuge to spin the filtered contents of the water, and reduced the contents to tiny pellets. Then they put the pellets in laboratory dishes and cultured them. Next, they examined the genes of any pathogens that grew, in order to identify the specific bacteria. This method enables the scientists to identify even a few bacteria in a sample of water as large as 10.5 quarts (10 L). With this level of accuracy, people can be better warned to stay away from waterways carrying infection and can protect themselves from disease.

few days before his illness struck. Because of Urbani's warning, hospitals in China instituted isolation procedures to prevent the spread of SARS. WHO named SARS the first global epidemic of the twenty-first century and issued a worldwide travel alert. The fast action was important everywhere because no treatment for SARS existed. More than 8,000 people were infected, and 774 died before isolation efforts slowed the spread of SARS and then stopped it in July 2003.

Paying the Ultimate Price for Research

Urbani was the first person to detect and identify SARS and to provide recommendations for preventing its spread, but he could not protect himself. The Hanoi hospital had a shortage of protective clothing. Urbani wore a mask to study the victims and their blood, but he had no goggles to protect his eyes or other clothing. He stayed at the hospital anyway for three weeks. On March 11, 2003, while on a flight to Thailand to meet with CDC researchers, he developed symptoms of the sickness. He knew what was happening. He made the doctor meeting him at the airport stay far away from him and sat in isolation in a far corner waiting for an ambulance. He insisted that the ambulance come with full protective gear. He called his wife and said, "Go back to Italy and take the children because this will be the end of me."[14] He died of SARS in the Thai hospital on March 29.

Urbani was praised by colleagues around the world for his sacrifice in the face of a public health emergency. One infectious disease researcher, Neal Halsey, says, "Everything Urbani did—the way he used his clinical expertise, the way he sounded the alarm, his willingness to ask for help—proved so, so important."[15] Protecting public health by identifying an unknown threat and preventing epidemics is a critical part of infectious disease research. Researchers know that SARS will not be the last mutated pathogen to pose a danger, and they strive to maintain continual vigilance against the peril of emerging new diseases.

enzyme

A protein produced by a cell which functions as a catalyst, causing chemical changes and reactions.

Treatment Research

Much of today's infectious disease treatment research concentrates on developing treatments for neglected diseases in the developing world. Researchers also want to develop new medicines for pathogens once thought conquered in the developed world that have now developed drug-resistant strains. No matter what the infection, says the Infectious Diseases Society of America, "Bad bugs need drugs."[16]

The Scourge of Sleeping Sickness

Sometimes the fight against "bad bugs," or pathogens, does not require new drugs but the development of a new way to use existing treatments. As a doctor with Médecins Sans Frontières (MSF), or Doctors Without Borders, Gerardo Priotto of Argentina saw a lot of suffering. He was especially disturbed during a trip to Uganda when he saw people dying of human African trypanosomiasis (HAT), commonly known as sleeping sickness. Sleeping sickness is caused by the bites of tsetse flies that carry the trypanosome parasite and pass it into a victim's blood. In the first stage of the disease, symptoms include bouts of fever, headaches, and joint pains. Then, in about 10 percent of victims, the parasite spreads to the central nervous system and the brain. This second stage can leave people paralyzed, mentally confused, and then comatose. It is fatal without treatment. Every year, WHO estimates, 50,000 to 70,000 people in Africa are infected with HAT. No one is sure how many die, because most victims live in poor, rural areas where accurate medical records are nonexistent.

Older drugs are available to treat HAT, but they are not satisfactory. One medicine, melarsoprol, was developed in 1949. It contains arsenic and is very toxic to people. The drug is so poisonous that it kills 1 of every 20 people treated with it. One MSF doctor has described the treatment this way: "It's a terrible drug—you don't feel proud injecting it. It is caustic, it burns them, and you don't know if you are going to save your patient or kill him."[17]

During the 1990s researchers discovered that a cancer drug called eflornithine could effectively kill sleeping sickness parasites, and doctors in Africa began using it in 2001. The drug is safer and less painful than melarsoprol, but treatment is difficult and requires the patient to be hospitalized. Eflornithine must be administered in intravenous injections given every six hours around the clock for 14 days. So few sleeping sickness victims could afford this treatment that 80 percent of patients were still being given melarsoprol. The answer, Priotto thought, must be finding the right combination of drugs to make treatment better. He said, "Due to its toxicity, we need to see a phasing out of melarsoprol as the primary drug for treating sleeping sickness."[18]

Research done in Africa, where sleeping sickness afflicts thousands of people every year, yielded a new treatment that is more practical and affordable than previous treatments. The disease is caused by the bite of the tsetse fly (pictured).

Research in the Field

In Africa, Priotto did not have a laboratory in which to test his combination treatment idea. Instead, in 2003 he began to do field research. He tested drug combinations right in the clinics where he worked. The field research was not easy. Sometimes patients simply left the hospital (and his study) because they could not afford to stay away from their villages and families anymore. Sometimes his research team did not understand the research rules and did not record results accurately. Priotto had to be flexible.

Finally, in 2004 Priotto was ready to do a study of hundreds of patients. He got help from MSF and from the US nonprofit organization Drugs for Neglected Diseases initiative (DNDi). He settled on two drugs as the best combination for treatment success: eflornithine and nifurtimox. Nifurtimox, which is given in tablets, is used in Central and South America to treat a parasitic illness called Chagas disease, which is similar to sleeping sickness. It is not a powerful drug. It kills the parasites of Chagas disease only about 70 percent of the time. Priotto determined, however, that combined with eflornithine, nifurtimox could reduce the time needed to treat sleeping sickness.

In 2009 he was able to report that his new treatment, called NECT, is just as effective as eflornithine therapy alone in curing sleeping sickness and is much more practical. NECT treatment still requires hospitalization, but it takes just 7 days, and the eflornithine is administered every 12 hours instead of every 6. Priotto says, "NECT shows just what we can do when we set our minds to improve patients' options, even in the most dire conditions."[19] Today, WHO has approved NECT for treating sleeping sickness and issues medical kits containing the necessary equipment and drugs to doctors working with HAT patients in Africa. It is not the perfect answer to treating sleeping sickness, but it is the quickest, most effective, and safest answer to be found so far.

> **intravenous injections**
>
> Treatment with drugs or other substances through a needle inserted into a vein.

Which Malaria Treatment?

Malaria is another parasitic tropical disease for which scientists needed to know which drug is best—especially in children. This question was the subject of a major international research study conducted between

Lethal Light

In 2009 a team of researchers at the New York Institute of Technology studied a new way to attack MRSA—it uses not drugs but a wavelength of blue light. In the laboratory, the scientists exposed two strains of *Staphylococcus aureus* to the light, which was filtered to avoid possibly dangerous ultraviolet waves. The process is called photo-irradiation. The team irradiated the bacteria with different doses of the blue light for varying lengths of time to see what worked best. The higher the dose, the more bacteria died, and at high doses, 90 percent of the bacteria were killed.

The scientists still do not know how blue light kills MRSA, but they believe that the process, which is both simple and inexpensive, could help to heal MRSA infections in people. It would not work for MRSA inside the body, but it could be used for skin infections and open MRSA wounds. The team also does not know whether MRSA could develop resistance to blue light, but at least the treatment could not cause antibiotic resistance to develop and would help prevent overuse of the latest antibiotics.

2005 and 2010. Four different species of the parasite *Plasmodium* cause the disease when people are bitten by infected mosquitoes. A person with malaria suffers fevers, chills, headaches, vomiting, and, when not treated, the death of red blood cells and then organ failure. Malaria kills about 1 million people around the world each year, and most of them are children under five years old or pregnant women. In the Western world and in Africa, malaria has been treated with the drug quinine, which kills the parasites. However, quinine is bitter-tasting, irritates the digestive system, can cause vomiting and diarrhea, and is fatal to young children in high doses. Sometimes it causes seizures, low blood sugar, and coma.

In Asia about 40 years ago, Chinese researchers began using a different medicine to treat malaria, one derived from an herb called sweet wormwood. The drug is called artesunate and is the treatment of choice in Asia. Chinese researchers insisted that artesunate is a better malaria drug than quinine, but Western and African doctors doubted its value. The medical community needed a definitive research study. In Africa, severe malaria continued to kill one in ten hospitalized children who were undergoing treatment.

An international team of researchers, led by infectious disease expert Nick White of the charitable organization Wellcome Trust, conducted a large study to compare the two drugs. The research was known as the African Quinine v. Artesunate Malaria Trial (AQUAMAT). Researchers studied 5,425 children hospitalized with severe malaria in nine African countries. They compared the outcomes of treatment with quinine versus treatment with artesunate. In 2010 AQUAMAT researchers reported 22.5 percent fewer deaths with artesunate than with quinine and fewer cases of seizures, low blood sugar, and coma. White says, "For over a century, quinine administered by injection has been the best treatment available for treating severe malaria, but thanks to the development of the artemisinin compounds [artesunate], we now have a safer and much more effective treatment. We recommend that artesunate should now replace quinine for the treatment of severe malaria in both children and adults everywhere in the world."[20] WHO now recommends artesunate as the treatment of choice for severe malaria.

The Problem of Treating Viral Infections

Infectious disease researchers have achieved valuable successes in the effort to develop better treatments for the parasites that cause malaria and sleeping sickness, but discovering new medicines for other deadly diseases is a harder task. Viruses, for instance, especially retroviruses such as HIV, can be extremely difficult to attack with medicines. For example, antibiotics work by killing bacteria, but antiviral drugs cannot kill viruses. Viruses live and reproduce inside host cells, so killing the virus would also kill the host cell. This would harm the infected person's body instead of healing it. HIV causes severe illness because it invades immune system cells. The immune system recognizes the invading viruses as foreign and sends immune cells to attack them, but the viruses latch onto the immune cells, take them over, and kill them. The death of immune system cells is what causes AIDS. No drug that kills immune system cells would help an infected person.

Because of this problem, the first antiviral drugs were developed much later than antibiotics. Antiviral medicines work to inhibit or slow the virus's ability to reproduce. Antiviral drugs do not cure disease, but they can slow its progression, sometimes for decades.

Attacking HIV in Different Ways

The first antiretroviral drug was approved for use against HIV infection in 1987. It is known as zidovudine, or AZT. It could delay AIDS from developing for about two years in people infected with HIV. Today, however, combinations of more than 20 different kinds of antiretroviral drugs can prevent infected people from getting AIDS for many years. Combinations are necessary because HIV mutates so easily that the virus can quickly become resistant to a single type of drug.

Protease inhibitors are one type of antiretroviral drugs developed in the 1990s. These drugs attack the enzyme in HIV called protease. HIV, explains AIDS advocate Martin Delaney, has a kind of life cycle in the human body that goes through several steps. The protease enzyme is made by the virus in one of the steps near the end of its life cycle. It marks the step at which the virus is replicating and making new copies of itself. Delaney says, "So protease inhibitor is a drug that inhibits, that stops that from happening, so that what comes out of the cell, rather than an organized, functional new copy of the virus is a bunch of jumbled genetic material."[21] In this state the virus cannot infect any new cells. Joseph A. Martin and Sally Redshaw, researchers at the Hoffman-LaRoche pharmaceutical laboratories, created the first protease inhibitor to treat HIV, named Invirase. Several different protease inhibitors are now available, and they are powerful, but HIV does become resistant to them.

> **protease inhibitors**
>
> Antiretroviral drugs used against HIV that block the action of the enzyme protease and thereby prevent replication of the virus in the cell.

In 2003 researchers developed enfuvirtide, an antiretroviral drug called a fusion inhibitor. It blocks the virus from fusing or joining with a host cell's wall so that it cannot slip inside and take over the cell's functions. Enfuvirtide was developed by researchers at the pharmaceutical companies Roche and Trimeris, and it works even when HIV has mutated and become resistant to other drugs.

A New Idea for Cell Protection

The newest antiretroviral drug for HIV was approved for use in 2007. It is called Maraviroc and is in a class of drugs called CCR5 antagonists. Discovered by a research team at the pharmaceutical company Pfizer, it works on immune cells instead of on the virus. The researchers identified

Fighting Fungi

Fungus infections, such as athlete's foot, thrush, ringworm, and other skin and nail infections can be very difficult to control. Only a few antifungal medicines are available, either as creams or as oral drugs. The creams are often too mild to heal the infection, but the drugs usually cause side effects, such as nausea and diarrhea. In addition, just like bacteria, pathogenic fungi can become resistant to medicines. New treatments are needed.

In 2011 Ligia Salgueiro and Eugenia Pinto of the University of Columbia in Portugal reported that they and their research team had found a promising treatment. The scientists purified lavender oil from the lavender shrub that grows in Portugal. They exposed pathogenic fungi to the lavender oil in their lab and discovered that it damaged the cell walls, or membranes, of the fungi and killed them. The researchers believe that lavender oil could be a breakthrough treatment for fungal infections. Pinto says, "In the last few years there has been an increase in the incidence of fungal diseases. . . . Unfortunately there is also increasing resistance to antifungal drugs. Research by our group and others has shown that essential oils may be cheap, efficient alternatives that have minimal side effects." Although their treatment has not yet been tested in people, the scientists believe that they have made a good start toward developing a powerful medicine that could heal many kinds of fungal infections.

Quoted in *Journal of Medical Microbiology*, "Lavender Oil Has Potent Antifungal Effect," Infection Research, February 15, 2011. www.infection-research.de.

the protein on immune system cells that HIV latches onto in order to slip inside and infect the cells. They figured out that medicines might latch onto this protein, too, and spent 11 years finding one that did. Most people with HIV are infected by a strain that latches onto the protein named CCR5. Maraviroc latches onto CCR5 so that HIV is blocked and cannot get into the cell. Maraviroc works even when the virus is resistant to other antiretroviral drugs. Many infectious disease researchers are excited by the discovery of this new class of AIDS drug. The Pharmaceutical Research and Manufacturers of America awarded the CCR5 researchers their 2010

Discoverers Award. One of the leaders of the Maraviroc research team, Tony Wood, says, "I feel incredibly privileged to be part of the team that was in the right place at the right time to convert science into something of value to mankind."[22]

Finding drug treatments for pathogens that easily develop resistance is a constant struggle for infectious disease researchers. The work to stay one step ahead of mutating viruses continues, but other researchers face the same problem with bacteria. Their research targets resistant bacteria that are immune to existing antibiotics.

Deadly, Drug-Resistant Bacteria

When Brock Wade was 9 years old, he fought a powerful bacterium that almost killed him. In August 2009 Brock fell off a scooter. He had scrapes and cuts on one leg, but the injury did not seem serious and appeared to heal. Sometime later, however, Brock began complaining about pain in his arm that kept getting worse. Then he began passing out. Brock's parents took him to his doctor who ordered a series of medical tests. The results were frightening. Brock had a methicillin-resistant *Staphylococcus aureus* (MRSA) infection. *Staphylococcus aureus* is a common pathogen that can cause a variety of infections from boils on the skin to sore throats to pneumonia to urinary tract infections. Since the development of antibiotics, strains of these bacteria have mutated and become resistant to methicillin—the penicillin-like antibiotic that used to be best for killing staph.

fusion inhibitor

A class of antiretroviral drug that works on the host cell to prevent HIV from fusing with and infecting it.

MRSA had invaded Brock's bloodstream through the injury on his leg. Cuts are the most common way that MRSA gets into the body. Some of Brock's bacteria had traveled to the bones in his shoulder, causing a bone infection called osteomyelitis. He was also in septic shock— an overwhelming infection from the bacteria in his blood that released toxins, reduced the blood supply to his organs, and dropped his blood pressure. His lungs and heart were filling with fluid, and he was close to death. Doctors put Brock on five different antibiotics, but they could not kill all the bacteria. The boy underwent five surgeries. Some were to drain the fluid buildup from his lungs so he could breathe. Others were to surgically remove the infected bone in his shoulder. Brock finally did recover, but he was left with a permanent reminder of his ordeal. His mother says, "He left the hospital with what looked like a shark bite missing from his arm."[23]

A Losing Battle with MRSA

Many MRSA victims are not as lucky as Brock. In 2008 the CDC reported that more people in the United States die from MRSA than die from AIDS. In that year, in the United States, 11,295 people died of AIDS. Jason Newland, an infectious disease specialist at the University of Missouri–Kansas City, reported in 2010 that MRSA is responsible for more than 18,000 deaths in the United States every year. Newland also says that the incidence of MRSA infections is increasing. He and a research team conducted a study of children

Medical researchers have been stymied in their efforts to find a treatment for infections caused by the deadly, drug-resistant bacteria MRSA. Abscess and swelling is visible in the hand of a patient with a MRSA infection.

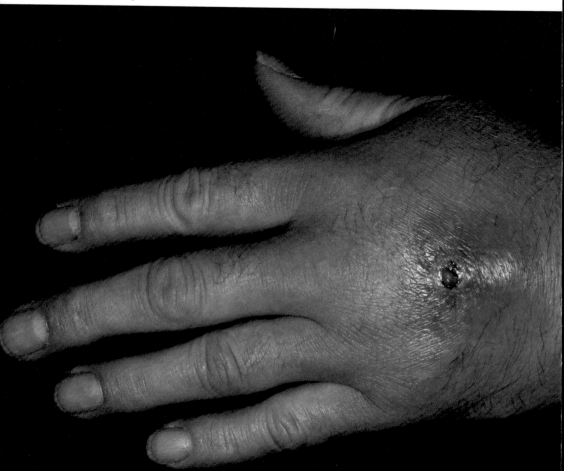

admitted to 25 different hospitals for MRSA infections between 1999 and 2008. They discovered that the hospitalizations for children with MRSA were 10 times higher in 2008 than in 1999. Julian Davies says that researchers trying to develop drugs to fight antibiotic resistant bacteria are in a "ceaseless, losing battle with microbes."[24] Nevertheless, researchers have kept trying to find the drug to which bacteria cannot develop resistance.

During the 1980s medical experts thought they had the answer to MRSA with an antibiotic called vancomycin. It was not often used until MRSA developed because it is so toxic to people. It can cause kidney damage and hearing loss in some users. Vancomycin fought MRSA successfully at first because the bacteria had not been previously exposed to it, but in 2002 vancomycin-resistant *Staphylococcus aureus* (VRSA) developed. That same year, researchers at Pfizer developed a new antibiotic named linezolid that worked in an entirely different way than previous antibiotics. This, they thought, might be the solution. Jessica Snyder Sachs explains that it "gummed up the bacterial cell's ability to make proteins."[25] Bacteria that cannot make proteins cannot survive or reproduce. The US Food and Drug Administration (FDA) approved the drug in 2002 and ordered that it be used only for MRSA and VRSA. Researchers at the FDA hoped that this order would prevent overuse of linezolid and bacterial resistance. But within a few years of the drug's introduction, the bacteria slowly mutated. Staph bacteria that are linezolid-resistant appeared in hospitals throughout the world by 2005.

Today, infectious disease experts recommend that all antibiotics be used sparingly to prevent bacteria from being exposed to them and evolving to resist them. Many kinds of bacteria have evolved into so-called superbugs that can resist all but one or two of the many antibiotics available today. Researchers fear that in time, bacteria that are resistant to every antibiotic will have evolved. They need to find new ways to kill bacteria and develop new kinds of super-antibiotics for superbugs. Some researchers are attacking the structure of bacterial cells; other researchers are infecting bacteria with viral diseases.

New Treatments for Evolving Enemies

Bacteria do have their own pathogens. Viruses that infect bacteria and make them sick are called bacteriophages. Infectious disease researcher

Mike Mattey and his team work in a company called Fixed Phage at the University of Strathclyde in Scotland. They have developed special bandages covered in bacteriophages that attack and kill the bacteria in skin infections. MRSA is responsible for many serious skin infections and wounds. The viruses grown by Fixed Phage are harmless to people but kill bacteria. Mattey explains how the bacteriophages work. He says, "If you imagine them as little hypodermic syringes which inject the cell— it's a nanotechnology, but a natural one. One bacteriophage will infect one bacterium, which then produces 50 more bacteriophages that will infect 50 bacteria and so on. It's very different [from] conventional treatment. . . . The more bacteria there are to kill, the better it works."[26] Fixed Phage's bacteriophage bandages became available for treating MRSA in 2011.

Bacteriophage bandages seem to work well for skin infections, but they cannot attack bacteria inside other organs. For that, new antibiotics that are swallowed or injected are necessary. Infectious disease researchers at Forest Laboratories in New York spent years developing a new kind of antibiotic for use against MRSA and VRSA. The new drug, called ceftaroline, is a broad-spectrum antibiotic, meaning that it kills several different kinds of bacteria, such as staph and streptococcus. The drug works by binding to proteins of the cell wall of the bacterium. This causes the cell wall to lose its normal structure. The wall gets too long and develops lesions, and finally the bacterium dies. Ceftaroline works to disorder cell wall structure in bacteria with various mutations, such as MRSA, because these bacteria have not developed a defense against it. The researchers conducted a series of trials with thousands of people hospitalized for serious, drug-resistant infections. They determined that their new drug was as good as older, more toxic drugs at destroying bacteria and was less likely to cause serious problems. It cured more patients than some of the older antibiotics, too. In 2010 the FDA approved ceftaroline for use in people with MRSA-caused pneumonia and skin infections.

bacteriophages

Viruses that infect bacteria.

Treatment Is an Unending Arms Race

FDA medical experts praised the new drug as a valuable and superior antibiotic for treating MRSA. For now, bacteria have no defense against ceftaroline, but experts know that eventually some bacteria will develop resistance to it. Forest Laboratories and the FDA recommend that the drug be used only for patients who are infected with resistant bacteria so that it will be useful as long as possible. But no drug is the one medicine to which bacteria will never develop resistance. Both viruses and bacteria always mutate over time in response to antimicrobial drug treatment. Perhaps, say many researchers, prevention—not treatment—is the real answer to infectious disease.

Prevention of Infectious Diseases

Ali Maow Maalin holds a unique place in the history of infectious disease. At age 23 he became the last person on Earth to catch naturally occurring smallpox. Smallpox is the first and, so far, the only infectious disease to be eliminated from the environment. Its eradication is a unique milestone in infectious disease prevention and was accomplished through a worldwide, intensive vaccination program.

Throughout the 1960s and 1970s, the UN Smallpox Eradication Unit, led by US physician Donald Henderson, had fanned out across Africa and Asia—the last areas of the world where smallpox was still a problem. The unit's ambitious goal was to vaccinate so many people that the smallpox virus, which infects only human hosts and has no other reservoir, would die out completely. Researchers tracked every reported or suspected case of infection. Medical workers vaccinated any person who had the slightest chance of contact with any infected individual. In 1977 Maalin, a Somali cook, was the last host of the dreaded disease. After Maalin recovered from his illness, the smallpox researchers monitored global reports of infections for two more years before they certified that smallpox had been eliminated in 1980.

The scientific triumph against smallpox illustrates the ultimate goal of infectious disease prevention efforts: disease eradication. But eradication is not always possible, and it is not the only means of prevention available to infectious disease researchers. Depending on the pathogen involved, prevention research might focus on vaccine development or it might target the vector, or carrier, of the pathogen. Other prevention researchers might target the environmental conditions that make it easy for the pathogen to infect people. And sometimes, their goal is to prevent infection by killing off the pathogen itself.

Targeting Guinea Worms

Infectious disease researchers are currently involved in a decades-long effort to rid the world of Guinea worm disease—an effort that began in the late 1980s. Guinea worms are large parasites that are endemic, or constantly present, in a region of Africa between the Sahara and the equator. The larvae of Guinea worms live in microscopic water fleas that infest stagnant ponds and water pools. People swallow the water fleas and Guinea worm larvae when they drink from these water sources. Inside the human body, a Guinea worm larva grows to be a long threadlike

A child from Congo (now Democratic Republic of the Congo) shows the telltale signs of smallpox in 1965, just 15 years before the disease was eradicated. Research into preventing and eradicating infectious diseases continues.

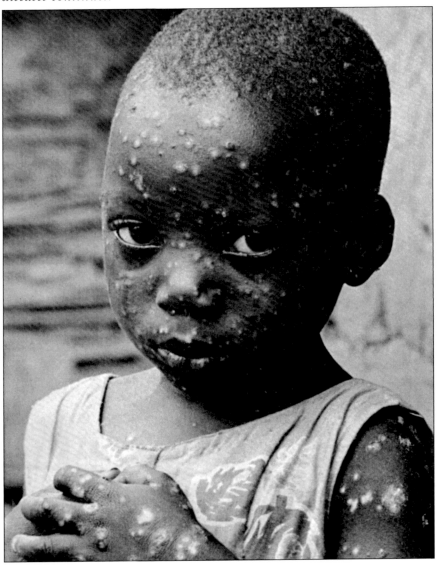

Success Is Never Guaranteed

In 2002 researchers with the pharmaceutical company GlaxoSmithKline began a final, large-scale study of a promising new vaccine to prevent herpes simplex infections. Two types of herpes simplex viruses exist: Type 1, or oral herpes, usually causes cold sores, and type 2 is the usual cause of genital herpes, a sexually transmitted disease. Both types are contagious, and in the United States about 20 percent of the population is infected with genital herpes, while more than 50 percent have been infected with the type 1 virus.

GlaxoSmithKline researchers developed a vaccine that protected against both types in laboratory and animal testing. The first human trials, however, demonstrated that the vaccine seemed to protect only women. It had no effect on men who were exposed to the herpes simplex virus through their infected sexual partners. The researchers did not know why this should be true, but the vaccine still appeared to be of great value for women. The researchers began an 8-year study of the vaccine's effectiveness with 8,323 women in the United States and Canada. It was to be the final trial of the vaccine before it was approved in the United States. In 2010, for reasons still unknown to the researchers, study results showed that the vaccine was a failure. It was completely ineffective at preventing herpes simplex infection in the women. Researchers continue to study the years of data in the hope of understanding what went wrong, but GlaxoSmithKline has abandoned efforts to develop the herpes vaccine for now.

worm about 2 to 3 feet (0.6 m to 0.9 m) long. About a year after initial infection, the worm penetrates the host's flesh and skin, usually at a leg or foot. The wound made by the Guinea worm causes burning pain, swelling, and lameness for the victim. One Nigerian sufferer, Hyacinth Igelle, says, "The pain is like if you stab somebody. It is like fire—it comes late, but you feel it even unto your heart."[27]

No medicine exists to treat this disease and no vaccine can prevent it. To soothe the pain, an infected person has few choices. Many plunge their affected limbs in cool water, and at that point the worm partially emerges and spews larvae out of the open sore. The larvae swim in the water till they are swallowed by water fleas, and anyone who drinks the water continues the Guinea worm life cycle of infection.

What Really Works?

Scientists hoping to prevent the spread of this terrible disease tried several approaches. They came up with a plan that included boring wells to provide clean drinking water, poisoning water fleas with chemicals added to ponds and pools, and teaching people not to drink from unclean water sources. As the Guinea Worm Eradication Program medical staff worked in the field, researchers with the program assessed the success and effectiveness of the interventions with surveys and field tests. Because of their ongoing research, the program leaders were able to determine how well the project was working and adjust their approach accordingly.

At first the scientists believed that the best prevention for Guinea worm disease would be the bored wells, but follow-up evaluations showed that this approach had limitations. In Ivory Coast, for example, where many wells were drilled, researchers discovered that initial success in reducing infections was only temporary. After a few years of use, the hand pumps for the wells broke, and people went back to drinking from contaminated water sources. The wells did not protect people who live a nomadic lifestyle in other countries either. As they moved from area to area, they often drank from unclean water sources. Even settled villagers sometimes reported drinking unclean water when they were, for instance, working in their fields and far away from the well.

eradication

Complete destruction or removal.

Chemical treatments of water pools turned out to be of questionable value, also. Although it killed the larvae in some areas, it did not work in other areas. In 2002 one researcher, O. Doumbo, reported that he had tested previously treated village ponds in Mali and often found that the treatment had not killed all the larvae. Other studies demonstrated that heavy rainfall soon after the water had been treated diluted the effectiveness of the chemicals. Both the chemical treatment of water sources and the bored wells had only mixed success.

Finding the Right Interventions

By the late 1990s researchers concluded that the best interventions were health education and providing personal water filters to people who had to use contaminated water sources. Scientists at the DuPont chemical company had earlier designed a cheap, usable filter for water fleas. They invented a tough, fine nylon mesh filter that people could pour drinking water through to strain out the water fleas. During the 1990s thousands of volunteers handed out millions of donated water filters to families living in thousands of remote villages in countries such as Nigeria, Burkina Faso, Togo, Sudan, and Mauritania that suffered repeated bouts of the disease. Program researchers went into villages and checked the percentage of households using the filters. They found that people liked them and that the majority used them regularly. One study discovered that the filters were so popular that even people who did not know filters could prevent Guinea worms used them.

Public health education also worked well for containing Guinea worm infections. This meant teaching people that Guinea worm disease comes from drinking unclean water and persuading them not to wash their wounds in drinking water sources. In one 2000 study of 160 villages in Sudan, for example, researchers found that incidences of Guinea worm disease had dropped from 4,177 to 515 in the year after educational programs were instituted.

As the project moved into the twenty-first century, the scientists had proof that their interventions were working. By 2010 Guinea worm disease was endemic in only four countries. The number of cases had dropped to about 1,700, as opposed to 3.5 million in 1986 when the eradication project began. The researchers with the project continue to study the effectiveness of their interventions and to monitor all countries where Guinea worm infections still occur. They will not certify that the disease has been eliminated until they are sure that no case is reported for three years. Nevertheless, says the Carter Center, which leads the Guinea Worm Eradication Program and provides its major funding, "Guinea worm disease is poised to be the next disease after smallpox to be eradicated."[28]

Killing the Carrier

Guinea worm disease research demonstrated that targeting the pathogen with public health measures was a viable method of prevention, but the prevention method has to be tailored to the disease. Today, researchers are working to prevent sleeping sickness (HAT) by targeting its vector—tsetse flies. Tsetse flies carry the infecting pathogen, and this parasite infects and kills animals such as antelopes, lions, and cattle, as well as people. The flies transmit the disease when they bite an infected host and then bite another person or animal. Preventing the disease in people, therefore, has no lasting effect, since the pathogen can move from animals back to people when the flies bite. Scientists believe that elimination or control of tsetse flies is probably the best prevention approach for sleeping sickness, but it is not an easy task. Tsetse flies are widespread in regions of Africa between the Sahara and Kalahari Deserts.

Initially, African countries and the United Nations attempted to eliminate tsetse flies by spraying insecticide over wide geographical areas, setting bait traps, and dipping livestock, such as cattle, in insecticide washes. These poisoning techniques reduced tsetse fly populations dramatically in many areas, but they did not kill all the tsetse flies. The fly population slowly recovered after an area was treated. Insecticides alone are not the answer to preventing sleeping sickness.

In 1995 scientists at the UN International Atomic Energy Agency (IAEA) offered another approach. They had learned how to use radiation

A medical technician in Ghana carefully pulls a Guinea worm from a patient's ankle, wrapping it around a moist bandage to keep it from breaking and causing infection. Scientists have spent decades on prevention and eradication of the painful Guinea worm disease.

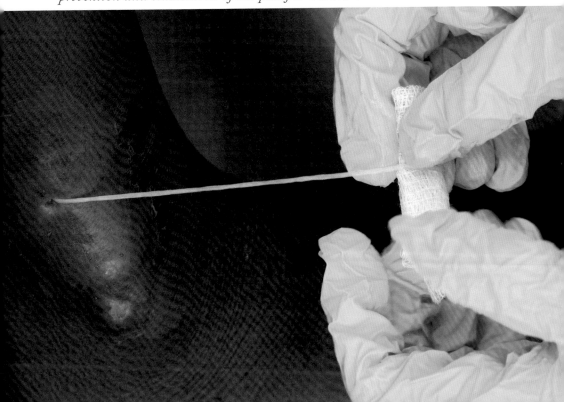

to make the flies sterile without otherwise harming them. Sterile flies can mate but cannot produce offspring, and this could eventually cause the flies to die out. To test this method, the researchers chose the island of Zanzibar, in Tanzania, for the study. As an island, it was like a natural laboratory where they had a discrete population of flies and could watch what happened to them. First, they used insecticides to reduce the fly population on the island. Then, the researchers used the Sterile Insect Technique (SIT) developed by the IAEA. In a laboratory, they raised large populations of captured tsetse flies. Then, the male tsetse flies were subjected to bursts of radiation that made them sterile. They would be able to mate, but they could not fertilize any females. The researchers released masses of the male tsetse flies into the air over Zanzibar. When enough sterile males populated the environment, the scientists predicted that the natural population would begin to die off.

For three years, they released sterile male tsetse flies over Zanzibar and conducted tests of the results. They used trapping techniques to count numbers of tsetse flies. They tested the blood of cattle for signs of infection and monitored people for symptoms. The SIT technique worked slowly, but it did work. In 2003 researchers, who were still monitoring Zanzibar, reported that no tsetse fly had been found for six years.

> **vector**
>
> The carrier that transfers a pathogen from one host to another.

Not Eliminated Yet

Because of the success of the Zanzibar study, the Organization of African Unity and WHO began the Pan African Tsetse and Trypanosomiasis Eradication Campaign (PATTEC) in 2001. Its goal is to use the SIT method to kill off and control tsetse flies and thus sleeping sickness in African areas where the disease is endemic. By 2009 PATTEC had succeeded in Namibia and Botswana and had greatly reduced populations in Nigeria, but tsetse flies remain a problem in several other African countries.

Some scientists believe that the SIT approach succeeded in Zanzibar only because it is an isolated island. They argue that on the mainland of Africa, too many flies exist in vast areas for it to work. Some even argue that eradicating tsetse flies is wrong because it changes the ecosystem. The head of PATTEC in Ethiopia, John Kabayo disagrees. He says that

Just a Simple Pill

In 2010 researchers led by the Gladstone Institutes of the University of California at San Francisco reported that they have evidence that a simple pill might prevent HIV infection. In a three-year study, the scientists gave half of 2,499 healthy homosexual men in six countries an antiretroviral drug, called Truvada, to take every day. The other half of the study participants were given a sugar pill for comparison. At the end of the study, cases of HIV infections in the men who faithfully took the drug every day were 90 percent fewer than in the sugar-pill group.

This was the first research to demonstrate that HIV infection could be prevented, not just slowed and treated, with an antiretroviral drug. Scientists are now conducting a larger study with about 20,000 other people, such as heterosexual men and women and drug-users who share needles. However, many scientists see no reason that the pill would not work as well for these people. Medical experts have called the pill's protection a major breakthrough in the fight against AIDS and a revolution in AIDS prevention.

SIT is the only demonstrated method so far that can give people hope of ridding themselves and their animals of sleeping sickness. If countries cooperate they might be able to control tsetse flies, but so far SIT methods have not been applied long enough and with the many millions of sterile flies needed for total elimination. PATTEC researchers continue, however, to evaluate the SIT method of controlling tsetse flies in Ethiopia, Kenya, and Mali, and they have not given up on the plan to eliminate them in the future.

Disease Prevention with Vaccines

Changing the environment by attacking the carrier is an ambitious method of preventing infectious disease that can depend on the political cooperation of many countries working together. It is a difficult and costly goal to achieve. Often, especially when the pathogen is a virus or a bacterium, a vaccine to protect an individual or a population from infection is the ideal prevention method for infectious disease. However, vaccine researchers face some complex issues, too. They have to determine the best strategy for prompting the immune system to produce antibodies against the infection.

Vaccine development strategies vary, depending on the pathogen involved. A weakened, live vaccine, for example, provokes the strongest antibody response, but some pathogens are so dangerous that even in a much weakened state, it is too risky to inject them into people and chance giving them the disease. Vaccines made of killed pathogens are safe, but the immune system may not make enough antibodies to provide immunity. Modern researchers have developed vaccines made just of parts or protein fragments of the pathogen. These vaccines, called subunit vaccines, are both safe and effective, but to develop them researchers have to determine exactly which protein fragment is the antigen that provokes the immune system to make antibodies. Identifying and isolating antigens can be a big problem for vaccine researchers.

> **endemic**
>
> Constantly present or prevalent in a locality, region, or people.

Despite the difficulties, researchers have developed vaccines against many diseases—from bacterial pneumonia to hepatitis—and dramatically reduced their threat in developed countries. Diseases that primarily affect people in developing countries, however, have often been neglected, in part because it is so expensive to develop new vaccines, in part because of the small worldwide demand for them, and in part because prevention presents complex development challenges. Scientists sometimes refer to these diseases as orphan diseases. At the Infectious Disease Research Institute (IDRI), a group of researchers and scientists is dedicated to the development of vaccines for some of the most neglected but devastating orphan diseases.

Leprosy: Treatment Is Not Enough

In partnership with American Leprosy Missions, IDRI researchers are involved in an intensive effort to develop a vaccine against leprosy, a neglected disease that cripples many people in the poorest areas of the world. Leprosy, or Hansen's disease, is caused by a bacterium that scientists believe is spread in droplets from the nose and mouth of infected people. The disease causes damage to the nerves, leading to numbness, weakness, and loss of sensation. Eventually, people with leprosy suffer disfiguring lesions and deformities, such as the loss of fingers, distorted facial features, and lumps and bumps on the skin, and are often shunned and rejected by their friends, family, and community. Mitano, a resident of the Democratic Republic of Congo, explains how devastating this social reaction to the disease can be. He says, "When I had leprosy, people abandoned me. Nobody wanted to shake my hands and share food with me. I was considered a non-human being."[29]

About 25 years ago, medical scientists learned to treat leprosy, stop its progression in the body, and render it noncontagious. Mitano's leprosy was cured with this treatment, but nothing could be done about the

A woman who is badly disfigured by leprosy (or Hansen's disease) visits with a Paraguayan official. Medical researchers are working on a vaccine for this ancient disease.

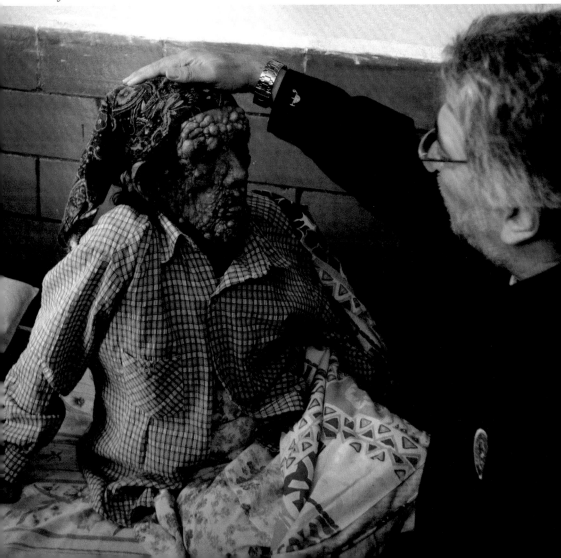

damage already done. Many leprosy victims have little access to treatment and may not even be diagnosed properly until they are deformed and crippled.

Therefore, according to IDRI, a vaccine is needed. The head of IDRI's leprosy research program, Malcolm Duthie, explains, "Our belief is that a vaccine will give an active protection. If we can vaccinate people, we could potentially break the transmission cycle."[30] Developing a vaccine for leprosy, however, is not easy. Leprosy is such a serious disease that using live bacteria is not an option. Killed leprosy bacteria cannot provoke a strong immune system response. Duthie and his team decided on a subunit vaccine, but the bacteria that cause leprosy are complex organisms with thousands of proteins on their cell surfaces. Identifying which proteins are the antigens that cause an antibody response has been time-consuming and difficult.

Since 2006 Duthie's team has been working in the laboratory to identify the important antigens of leprosy bacteria and develop a subunit vaccine. By 2010, using animals to test vaccine preparations, the team believed they had succeeded. They had identified leprosy antigens that caused an antibody response in the animals. They had developed a vaccine that they believe is safe but effective against leprosy infection. IDRI expected to begin testing the new vaccine in humans in 2011. If the trials succeed, leprosy may finally be conquered.

Public Health Prevention Strategies

Many, if not most, infectious diseases cannot be prevented with vaccines or eliminated in a population. The pathogens mutate or live in a variety of animal and human hosts and will always be a part of human life. Epidemiologists and public health researchers work to prevent these diseases by understanding how the diseases are transmitted in a population and how they are spread from person to person.

This is how MRSA, for example, is targeted today. Researchers realized that the bacteria were mutating because they were continually exposed to antibiotics and developed resistance. They determined that the antibiotics used to keep farm animals healthy were contributing to the development of resistant bacteria in human populations. They studied infection-control policies in hospitals and found that many hospital personnel did not wash their hands frequently or use good sanitation procedures. These studies led to recommendations for ways to decrease the spread of MRSA. For instance, many researchers lobby the government to regulate the use of antibiotics in animals. Doctors resist giving patients antibiotics unless absolutely necessary. Hospitals institute rigid infection control policies for all the staff. Patients are even encouraged to ask staff members to wash their hands before examining or treating them.

The First Step: Knowing Why

In New Zealand, public health researchers tried to solve another mystery. They wanted to know why some natives of the country, particularly the indigenous peoples known as Maoris and Pacific Islanders, have such a high rate of acute rheumatic fever. Rheumatic fever is caused by strep bacteria. Usually, the bacterium causes sore throat, but with rheumatic fever it goes on to attack other parts of the body and cause arthritis and heart damage. Because of antibiotics, cases of acute rheumatic fever are rare in the populations of most developed countries—except in Polynesians and Maoris. No one knew why these people were the exception, although researchers speculated it was a result of poverty and failure to seek medical treatment.

subunit vaccines

Vaccines made of proteins stripped from a pathogen, so that the vaccines contain antigens but nothing that can harm or infect a person.

In 2010 New Zealand researchers Richard Jaine and Michael Baker reported that cultural differences might account for the high incidence of acute rheumatic fever in these two populations. The researchers studied 1,249 case records of rheumatic fever between 1996 and 2005. They used census records to compare conditions in the homes of infected people. They discovered that members of extended families often share one home in Maori and Polynesian communities and that often several people share a bedroom. The research shows, say the scientists, that prevention of rheumatic fever may not depend on persuading people to seek prompt treatment for strep infection. Instead, Jaine argues, the research suggests that public health interventions and social programs that provide affordable housing to reduce the practice of overcrowding are the solution to preventing this infectious disease.

Prevention of infectious disease is rarely in the hands of researchers alone. If they develop a new vaccine, they still depend on society to accept and distribute it. If they develop a method to attack a vector, they may have to wait for governments to financially support the plan. And if they discover public health prevention methods, they must persuade social agencies or people themselves to institute the recommended interventions. In a sense, infectious disease researchers are just one part of a team effort to prevent the infectious diseases of the world.

What Is the Future of Infectious Disease Research?

n December 2008 doctors with Médecins Sans Frontières faced a dangerous crisis. In an isolated geographical area of the Western Kasai Province of the Democratic Republic of Congo, people were dying. The first reported death occurred on November 27 of that year. Then, on December 25 another man died; on December 28 a woman died with the same symptoms. By December 31 MSF doctors had 38 suspected cases of the same infectious disease—Ebola virus. Of those 38 victims, 12 eventually died, even with the best hospital care that MSF could provide. Ebola virus causes high fever, headache, diarrhea, and vomiting when the disease first begins. Then, as the disease progresses, the viruses attack the cells of blood vessels, causing them to leak and bleed. People vomit blood from the stomach and have bloody diarrhea from intestinal breakdown. They bleed from the eyes, ears, and nose. Their bodies go into shock, and death is likely. No medication has been found to treat Ebola fever, and no vaccine to prevent its spread has been discovered.

Death rates for infected populations range from 50 to 90 percent. MSF doctors were able to stop the epidemic only by isolating suspected cases, isolating people who had been in close contact with victims, and practicing sanitation and sterilization procedures. They provided supportive care for their patients, meaning such treatments as IV fluids to prevent dehydration and providing oxygen.

Emerging and Reemerging Diseases

MSF medical personnel were able to stop the epidemic from advancing, but it was neither the first nor last outbreak of the disease in this area or in other areas of Africa. Two villages in Uganda had an Ebola epidemic in 2007, and the Western Kasai Province had another Ebola outbreak in 2009. The very first known outbreaks of Ebola occurred in 1976 in

Scientists in Ivory Coast bag the skull of a colobus monkey for testing as part of research into the source of Ebola virus. Ebola fever is a devastating illness for which no treatment or vaccine yet exists.

the Democratic Republic of Congo and in Sudan. Since that time about 1,850 cases of Ebola have been identified, with more than 1,200 deaths. Ebola is an emerging disease. An emerging disease is one that appears without warning in a population. In the case of Ebola, scientists believe that it is an infection of nonhuman primates, such as chimpanzees, monkeys, and gorillas, which originally may have been infected by fruit bats. A human in close contact with an infected primate catches it and then spreads it to other people through bodily fluids, such as vomit, feces, urine, saliva, or tears. With an emerging disease, researchers must identify the pathogen, determine how it is spread, and then work to develop medicines or vaccines that successfully treat or prevent it.

Emerging diseases are the focus of intense research around the world, and scientists hope to develop effective weapons against them in the future. They have the same goal with reemerging diseases, such as TB, that were once decreasing and now are making a comeback—perhaps because of drug resistance or because they were never conquered. The emergence of new diseases, age-old diseases for which there are no effective cures, and the development of drug-resistant microbial strains are a global problem, and infectious disease researchers are committed to developing new drugs and vaccines to fight them. Some of these diseases, such as Ebola, are rare, but others, such as AIDS, are universal threats that infect millions every year.

Antibiotic Plan Required

David Gilbert of the Infectious Diseases Society of America (IDSA) is particularly concerned about drug-resistant bacteria and the need for new antibiotics to fight them. He says, "Prior generations gave us the gift of antibiotics. Today, we have a moral obligation to ensure this global treasure is available for our children and future generations."[31]

In 2004 the IDSA produced a report describing the crisis of antibiotic-resistant diseases and the failure of researchers to develop new antibiotics. In part, the crisis exists because producing antibiotics is not profitable for pharmaceutical companies. In part, it exists because federal governments have not financially supported research into new antibiotics and make it very difficult for drug companies to get new drugs approved. In part, it exists because scientists and the public have taken a long time to recognize that drug-resistant bacteria are a serious threat to the world. In 2010 an IDSA news release argued, "Resistant organisms will continue to develop in perpetuity, so we must have a plan in place to replenish our arsenal of drugs into the foreseeable future." It says that researchers and drug companies must be able to "deliver new antibiotics on an ongoing basis."[32]

emerging disease

A new infection in a population caused by the evolution of or change in a pathogen.

So far, the goals of IDSA have not been met. In 2002, for example, 89 new drugs were approved by the FDA, and none were antibiotics. Between 2003 and 2007 only four new antibiotics got FDA approval. From 2008 to 2010 only two antibiotics were approved. The IDSA has begun a campaign called the 10x20 Initiative that calls for 10 new antibiotics by 2020. Many researchers insist the goal is impossible, if only because after years of research in the laboratory, many antibiotic preparations turn out not to work as well for people as for animals or are discovered to have serious side effects. But IDSA insists that with pharmaceutical commitment and government help, it can be done.

Toward a New Antibiotic

Researchers at some drug companies are trying to meet the need for new antibiotics. At Optimer Pharmaceuticals in San Diego, a scientific team led by Sherwood Gorbach has developed a new antibiotic, fidaxomicin, to treat a type of serious diarrhea caused by the bacterium *Clostridium difficile*. This infection is difficult to treat without harming the good bacteria in people's intestines. It also has developed into a new, drug-resistant strain. In 2011 researchers at Optimer joined with researchers in Canada to test their new drug in patients with *Clostridium difficile* infections. With 629 people, they tried the new drug for half of them and an older antibiotic for the other half. Fidaxomicin worked even better than the older drug, and it specifically killed the infecting bacteria while leaving good intestinal bacteria unharmed. One medical doctor commented about the trial results, "This is a major advance."[33]

Fidaxomicin is not yet available to the public because it has not been approved by the FDA, but Optimer has asked the FDA to put it on the fast-track for approval. Fast-track FDA approval is one way the government can encourage the development of new drugs. It is an approach that expedites investigation of a drug and its safety and gets it to the market quickly. If fidaxomicin is fast-tracked, it could be approved in just a few months instead of the years that are usually needed for approval. That could mean a new antibiotic treatment for the approximately 3 million people in the United States who suffer this infection every year.

Thwarting Resistance

The charitable foundation Wellcome Trust is funding research at the British drug company Phico Therapeutics that could lead to a new kind of antibiotic that may be able to fight the problem of drug resistance. The antibiotic is a virus, a bacteriophage, which is altered in the laboratory. It injects a gene for making special proteins into bacteria such as *Staphylococcus aureus* and MRSA. The gene takes over the bacterial DNA and instructs the bacterium to make proteins that

A TB Vaccine

Researchers have found it very challenging to develop a vaccine against the complex bacterium that causes tuberculosis (TB). In the lungs, the bacterium actually attacks immune system cells and destroys them. The hard, waxy shell of the bacterium protects it and hides the many antigens both from the immune system and from researchers. However, in 2010 scientists in India succeeded in making a detailed map of the entire genetic structure of the bacterium's 4,000 genes. In partnership, researchers at GlaxoSmithKline and the Infectious Disease Research Institute succeeded in mapping all the antigens on the bacterium's surface.

With this knowledge, the partnership was able to develop a laboratory vaccine with particular kinds of antigens. Because the tuberculosis bacterium can kill some immune system cells, the antigens are ones that provoke a special kind of immune fighter called a T cell. Some kinds of T cells stimulate antibody production and others are killer cells that destroy invaders. For TB, T cells must be activated for a good immune system response. The new vaccine is made of antigens that stimulate T cells. In laboratory animals, it has successfully protected against TB infection, but the research has a long way to go. With humans, the vaccine is in only the first phase of tests. Nevertheless, the researchers are hopeful that their new understanding of the bacterium's antigens has led them to a vaccine that will someday end the threat of TB.

bind to its DNA and switch it off. With its DNA turned off, the bacterium cannot feed or multiply. The most important thing about the drug protein is that it can bind anywhere on the whole strand of bacterial DNA and destroy its ability to function. So, the researchers think, bacteria cannot develop resistance to the drug. Even if mutated strains of bacteria develop different DNA instructions, they will not have evolved to become resistant. The drug will simply target another point on the DNA strand.

Using a drug to change a bacterium's genes and DNA is new technology that has never been accomplished successfully before. Although the antibiotic works in the laboratory, Phico researchers are just beginning to test the drug on people. Their first test, completed in 2010, involved giving the antibiotic to 46 healthy people and provided them with initial evidence that the drug was safe for humans. Now, they are testing it in a small number of infected people to see if it works to destroy their bacteria. It will be years before the antibiotic is ready for use in the general population, but if it works, researchers believe that they will have an antibiotic that is able to target many kinds of bacteria.

Learning to Know the Enemy

At the Los Alamos National Laboratory, other researchers are also studying the genetic makeup of bacterial cells in order to develop new kinds of antibiotics. The researchers do not have an antibiotic to test yet. Instead, they are using a New Mexico supercomputer to understand exactly how the ribosomes in a living bacterial cell function. Ribosomes are the protein factories of cells and are made of strands of RNA. A ribosome looks like a snarled tangle of rubber bands that swivel and flow as they make new chains of proteins for the cell.

ribosomes

The components of cells in all living organisms that make proteins. They are the cell's machines that are responsible for translating the genetic coding to produce the proteins needed for growth, function, and reproduction.

In 2010 the Los Alamos researchers used bacteria that thrive in very hot conditions to observe the behavior of ribosomes. They flash froze the bacteria at different stages of ribosome movement in building new cell proteins. They examined the different frozen stages under a powerful electron microscope and then fed the results into the supercomputer. The supercomputer then built a model that creates a series of molecular pictures or snapshots that show the motion of a ribosome as it builds its protein.

All of this complex work may someday pay off in the development of new antibiotics that target bacterial ribosomes and disrupt their normal motion. However, this research is just the first step. One scientist, Janna Wehrle, explains, "While static images of the ribosome have revealed the detailed structure of the complex, we still don't know how all the parts of the machine work together to make proteins." But she believes that the research is the beginning of "offering a new way to target harmful, multi-drug resistant bacteria."[34]

With new knowledge of the ways that bacteria function and multiply, researchers hope that new kinds of antibiotics that can keep drug-resistant bacteria under control will be developed in the future. IDSA scientists have identified six super-resistant bacteria, most of which threaten hospitalized patients, as critical targets for research. Currently, these six pathogens cause the majority of hospital infections around the world and are each resistant to several antibiotics. Unless new antibiotics are developed, the young people of today will have no protection against these dangerous pathogens in the future.

Antiviral Drug Research and Ebola

Antiviral drugs are even more difficult to develop than antibiotics, but today, infectious disease researchers are making progress against the deadly Ebola virus for which no treatment currently exists. Some of this research targets the genetic material of viruses, just as scientists target the genes of bacteria. For example, Thomas Geisbert and his team at the National Emerging Infectious Diseases Laboratories Institute at Boston University School of Medicine are targeting the viruses' RNA. In the laboratory, the team developed a medicine made of tiny particles of genetic substances called "small interfering RNAs." They are absorbed by the viruses and disrupt their own RNA and thus their ability to reproduce. First, the researchers tested the treatment in guinea pigs and then in monkeys, which are more similar to humans. Even when given massive doses of Ebola—30,000 times more than should have killed them—the treated monkeys survived. Geisbert knows that the road ahead is a long one before the treatment can be approved for infected humans, but he says it is a major step in the right direction. He states, "We believe this work justifies the immediate development of this treatment as an agent to treat EBOV [the deadliest strain of Ebola]-infected patients."[35]

Scientists at the Rega Institute for Medical Research in Belgium are also studying Ebola treatment possibilities. They discovered that purified and chemically altered simple sugar molecules can fight the pathogen. The scientists are still working with animals in the laboratory to test their treatment and understand how it works, but by 2010 they reported promising results. In their study, they infected mice with Ebola and then gave half the mice their purified compound made of sugar. In these treated mice, 90 percent survived the infection. The researchers believe that the compound works by speeding up the immune system's response to the viruses. The immune system blocked the viruses before they entered and destroyed the victim's cells. John Wherry, the editor of the science journal that reported the results, says, "This is an exciting discovery because it offers hope that we will finally be able to really do something about some of the world's deadliest viruses—rapidly mobilizing antiviral immune cells is critical in the race between these killer viruses and the host."[36]

Protection Against HIV

Using the immune system to fight pathogens is also the goal of vaccine researchers. These infectious disease scientists hope to end the threat of deadly diseases by preventing people from ever becoming infected. Development of an AIDS vaccine, for instance, is the target of the International AIDS Vaccine Initiative. The organization says that an AIDS vaccine is desperately needed. Despite the availability of antiretroviral drugs, AIDS still threatens millions of people around the world. The International AIDS Vaccine Initiative website states, "For every two people who gain access to antiretroviral drugs today, five are newly infected by the virus."[37] Because HIV mutates so rapidly, the major problem for researchers is finding a vaccine that can protect people against all the varying strains, or subtypes.

subtypes

Distinct strains of microorganisms that are classified according to their genetic variations but are all descended from the same type, such as HIV.

An effective vaccine has to provoke an antibody response from the immune system to all or most of the subtypes. This means, for researchers, finding antibodies that broadly respond to many types of HIV. Scientists feel sure that such antibodies exist, but identifying them has been very difficult. They have to find the particular antigens that all the HIV strains have in common in order to develop a vaccine that will provoke the correct antibodies to fight the viruses. With most diseases at least a few people survive their infections, and scientists can examine their blood to see which antibodies successfully fought off the pathogens. With AIDS, however, no one's immune system has ever fought off the virus and eliminated it. For years, AIDS researchers have searched for the antibodies that can point the way to the antigens that would make an effective vaccine.

The first breakthrough came in the fall of 2009. Dennis Burton of the Scripps Research Institute in California was examining a blood sample from an HIV-positive man in Africa and found two new "super-antibodies." In subsequent studies, Burton discovered that these antibodies could neutralize the viruses by preventing them from slipping inside a cell. Most important, they blocked about 80 percent of the HIV subtypes. Then, in 2010 government researchers at the Vaccine Research Center of the National Institute of Allergy and Infectious Diseases (NIAID) discovered two more antibodies in the blood of an HIV-positive African American. These antibodies neutralized 90 percent of HIV subtypes by preventing HIV from entering a cell. The African man and the African American man were infected with different HIV sub-

HIV particles (yellow) bud from the membrane of a host cell (blue) in this colored scanning electron micrograph. Efforts to develop a vaccine against HIV/AIDS have been complicated by the speed with which HIV mutates.

types. So far, these antibodies have been tested only in dishes in the lab, but Burton hopes to begin studying the effects of his antibodies in animals sometime soon.

Anthony Fauci, the director of NIAID, is excited by the antibody discoveries. He explains, "The two sets of antibodies target different regions of the virus-cell interface—together they could help scientists develop a formidable vaccine against AIDS. The strategy is going to be to put the best antibodies together, and you are going to have a whopper against HIV."[38] Much more research is needed before an AIDS vaccine becomes a reality, but a vaccine that protects against 90 percent or more of HIV subtypes could save millions of lives.

The First Vaccine for a Parasite

A vaccine to prevent malaria would also be a lifesaver. Malaria researchers imagine a future world where this ancient enemy finally is conquered. No one has ever developed a vaccine against a parasite, but a malaria vaccine will probably be the first. Researchers at the drug company Glaxo-SmithKline are in the final testing stage of a new malaria vaccine. The challenge of malaria is the complex life cycle of the parasite, which means different antibodies are needed at different stages of the pathogen's life.

adjuvant

A substance added to a vaccine that stimulates and enhances immune system response.

When the malaria parasite is first injected into a victim through a mosquito bite, it travels in the bloodstream until it reaches the liver. There, it grows, multiplies, and changes into a new form. The new forms go on to infect red blood cells, and at this stage, the disease causes illness and death. GlaxoSmithKline's new vaccine targets the liver stage of the disease, before damage is done. The vaccine is made of proteins that are the antigens of the liver form of the parasite. The proteins are combined with an adjuvant, a chemical that encourages and boosts immune system response.

After 10 years of research with volunteers in Africa, GlaxoSmith-Kline researchers found that the vaccine could reduce actual episodes of malarial sickness in children by 50 percent. It could not prevent infection nor prevent the blood form of the parasite, but it could prevent, at least half the time, the liver stage from developing into the blood stage. The vaccine may not offer perfect protection, but it would save many children from dying of malaria.

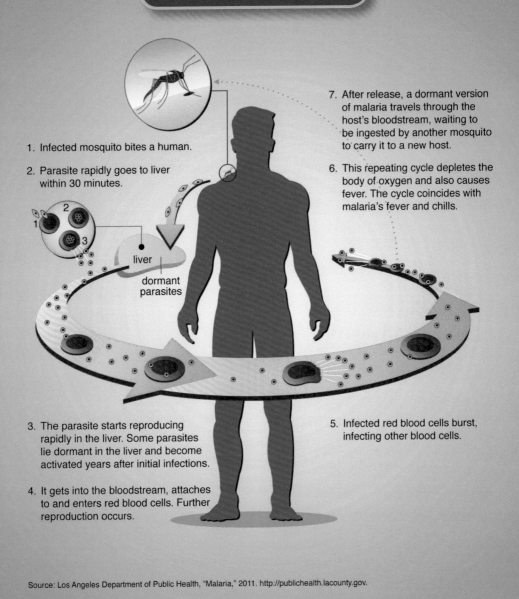

How Malaria Spreads

1. Infected mosquito bites a human.

2. Parasite rapidly goes to liver within 30 minutes.

3. The parasite starts reproducing rapidly in the liver. Some parasites lie dormant in the liver and become activated years after initial infections.

4. It gets into the bloodstream, attaches to and enters red blood cells. Further reproduction occurs.

5. Infected red blood cells burst, infecting other blood cells.

6. This repeating cycle depletes the body of oxygen and also causes fever. The cycle coincides with malaria's fever and chills.

7. After release, a dormant version of malaria travels through the host's bloodstream, waiting to be ingested by another mosquito to carry it to a new host.

liver

dormant parasites

Source: Los Angeles Department of Public Health, "Malaria," 2011. http://publichealth.lacounty.gov.

In 2009 the last required stage of testing, called the Phase III trial, began with 16,000 children in seven African countries. It is the largest drug trial ever conducted in Africa and will continue through 2012. Says the vaccine's codeveloper, Joe Cohen, "This is a tremendous moment in the fight against malaria. . . . The Phase III trial is

Anthony Fauci

Anthony Fauci is the director of the National Institute of Allergy and Infectious Disease (NIAID). Fauci grew up in New York City, living in an apartment above his family's drugstore. He enjoyed sports and games, but he also liked puzzles, science, and asking questions. When he grew up, he went to medical school, and as a new doctor during the late 1960s, he realized that he wanted to work in public health and help people. He joined NIAID and became the director in 1984.

Between 1981 and 1984 he faced the greatest puzzle of his life. It was AIDS, and neither he nor anyone else understood what it was. Eventually, he came to be an expert on AIDS and how it destroys the immune system. In 1984, however, Fauci faced protests and demonstrations from desperate people who blamed him for the government's failure to help AIDS victims. He invited the protesters into his office and listened to their concerns.

By the 1990s he and his NIAID team began searching for a cure, and although that goal has not been achieved, AIDS is now a manageable disease. Between 1999 and 2006 Fauci was the world's 10th most cited researcher in the field of AIDS because he had published so many important research results about the disease. Today, he continues to research HIV/AIDS as well as to educate the public about disease threats.

a huge undertaking that depends on effective coordination between researchers, regulators, families and communities. Everyone involved has invested significant energy and resources to pave the way for what could become the world's first malaria vaccine."[39] If the trial is successful in proving safety and effectiveness, the vaccine could be available within three to five years.

Preventing Infections, One Disease at a Time

Vaccines against other deadly infectious diseases, such as tuberculosis, *Clostridium difficile*, and leishmaniasis are currently being tested in laboratories and with small groups of human volunteers at various locations worldwide. The researchers believe that someday, safe, effective vaccines could make those diseases as rare as measles, polio, and chickenpox are now in developed countries. Vaccines may also be the answer to the problem of antibiotic-resistant bacteria, since prevention makes treatment unnecessary. In humankind's eternal war against pathogens, researchers struggle to win each battle, one infectious disease at a time.

Source Notes

Introduction: Devastating Diseases

1. Sunil Sazawal, "Faculty Directory," Johns Hopkins University. http://faculty.jhsph.edu.

2. Infection Research, "Infectious Diseases." www.infection-research.de.

Chapter One: What Is Infectious Disease Research?

3. Jessica Snyder Sachs, *Good Germs, Bad Germs: Health and Survival in a Bacterial World*. New York: Hill and Wang, 2008, p. 17.

4. Quoted in Sachs, *Good Germs, Bad Germs*, p. 20.

5. Quoted in Bob Weintraub, *Paul Ehrlich (1854–1915) and the Hebrew University*, Chemistry.org, p. 24. http://chemistry.org.il.

6. Quoted in Felissa R. Lashley and Jerry D. Durham, eds., *Trends and Issues: Emerging Infectious Diseases*. New York: Springer, 2007, p. xvii.

7. F. Gonzalez-Crussi, foreword to *The Woman with a Worm in Her Head & Other True Stories of Infectious Disease* by Pamela Nagami, New York: St. Martin's Griffin, 2001, p. viii.

8. Julian Davies, "Where Have All the Antibiotics Gone?," *Canadian Journal of Infectious Diseases and Medical Microbiology*, vol. 17, no. 5, pp. 287–90, September/October 2006; reprint, Pulsus Group, PubMed Central. www.ncbi.nlm.nih.gov.

Chapter Two: Identification and Diagnosis Research

9. Quoted in Nagami, *The Woman with a Worm in Her Head*, p. 180.

10. Nagami, *The Woman with a Worm in Her Head*, p. 189.

11. Quoted in Seth Augenstein, "DNA Test Developed by UMDNJ Researcher May Revolutionize Tuberculosis Diagnosis, Treatment," *Newark (NJ) Star-Ledger*, December 10, 2010. www.nj.com.

12. Quoted in Augenstein, "DNA Test Developed by UMDNJ Researcher May Revolutionize Tuberculosis Diagnosis, Treatment."

13. Quoted in *International Business Times*, "New Test Can Detect TB in Two Hours," September 2, 2010. www.ibtimes.com.

14. Quoted in Vernon Lee, "Tribute to Dr. Carlo Urbani, Identifier of SARS," SARS Info Center. www.bikesutra.com.

15. Quoted in Jim Duffy, "Anatomy of an Epidemic," *Johns Hopkins Public Health*, Fall 2003. www.jhsph.edu.

Chapter Three: Treatment Research

16. Infectious Diseases Society of America, home page. www.idsociety.org.

17. Quoted in Médecins Sans Frontières, "Sleeping Sickness," Campaign for Access to Essential Medicines, 2006. www.msfaccess.org.

18. Quoted in Médecins Sans Frontières, "New Study Shows Potential for Shorter and Safer Sleeping Sickness Treatment," press release, November 15, 2006.

19. Quoted in Sadia Kaenzig, "Profile: Gerardo Priotto," *DNDi Newsletter*, November 2008. www.dndi.org.

20. Quoted in *Drug Discovery and Development Magazine*, "Call for Change to Treatment for Severe Malaria," November 8, 2010. www.dddmag.com.

21. Martin Delaney, "Interview: Martin Delaney," *Frontline*, transcript, PBS, December 4, 2004. www.pbs.org.

22. Quoted in PRN Newswire–US Newswire, "Scientists Honored with Discoverers Award for Development of Innovative HIV Medicine Maraviroc," March 18, 2010. www.hivdent.org.

23. Ronda Bailey-Wade, "Brock Wade's Story," Infectious Diseases Society of America (IDSA), August 2010. www.idsociety.org.

24. Davies, "Where Have All the Antibiotics Gone?"

25. Sachs, *Good Germs, Bad Germs*, p. 119.

26. Quoted in Andrew Czyzewski, "Dressing Harnesses Viruses to Combat Bacterial Infection," *Engineer*, January 25, 2011. www.theengineer.co.uk.

Chapter Four: Prevention of Infectious Diseases

27. Quoted in Donald G. McNeil Jr., "Dose of Tenacity Wears Down an Ancient Horror," *New York Times*, March 26, 2006. www.cartercenter.org.

28. The Carter Center, "Guinea Worm Disease Eradication." www.cartercenter.org.

29. Quoted in American Leprosy Missions, "Your Compassion Transformed This Outcast's Life," Stories of Your Gifts at Work. www.leprosy.org.

30. Quoted in Rachel Solomon, "Seattle Scientist Works to Develop New Leprosy Vaccine," *Seattle Times*, August 1, 2010. http://seattletimes.nwsource.com.

Chapter Five: What Is the Future of Infectious Disease Research?

31. Quoted in IDSA, "ID Physicians Call for 10 New Antibiotics by 2020," news release, March 16, 2010. www.idsociety.org.

32. IDSA, "ID Physicians Call for 10 New Antibiotics by 2020."

33. Quoted in Kathleen Doheny, "New Antibiotic Fights *C. diff* Infections," WebMD Health News, February 2, 2011. www.rxlist.com.

34. Quoted in News-Medical.net, "Research on Ribosome Could Aid Antibiotic Development Against MRSA Infection," Medical News, December 3, 2010. www.news-medical.net.

35. Quoted in redOrbit, "Breakthrough Research for Fighting the Ebola Virus," May 28, 2010. www.redorbit.com.

36. Quoted in Federation of American Societies for Experimental Biology, "Sweet Discovery Raises Hope for Treating Ebola, Lassa, Marburg and Other Fast-Acting Viruses," ScienceDaily, November 4, 2010. www.sciencedaily.com.

37. International AIDS Vaccine Initiative, "Recent Progress in AIDS Vaccine Science." www.iavi.org.

38. Quoted in Alice Park, "AIDS Vaccine: The Promise of HIV Antibodies," *Time*, July 10, 2010. www.time.com.

39. Quoted in GlaxoSmithKline, "World's Largest Malaria Vaccine Trial Now Underway in Seven African Countries," press release, November 3, 2009. http://us.gsk.com.

Facts About Infectious Disease Research

Bacteria

- Approximately 100 billion bacteria (mostly harmless) live on a human's skin. If they could all be balled up together, they would fit into a pea.
- About 15 trillion beneficial, or friendly, bacteria are residents of the human intestinal tract. Gathered together, they would fill a soup can.
- Humans require beneficial bacteria to digest food, and antibiotics kill beneficial bacteria in the intestinal tract along with infecting pathogens. This is why people often get diarrhea after a course of antibiotics; the beneficial bacteria have not recovered from the attack.
- According to the CDC, approximately 2 million Americans carry MRSA in their noses, but in most people it does no harm.

Viruses

- The viral illness measles is the most contagious disease known to humankind.
- Only about 30 percent of the bacteria on Earth are pathogenic, but most viruses are harmful to their hosts and cause disease.
- Viruses are usually between 20 and 250 nanometers in size. For comparison, the diameter of a human hair is about 50,000 nanometers.
- Once inside a host cell, one virus can replicate, explode out of the cell, infect more cells, and become a million viruses in just a few hours.

Parasites

- The World Health Organization (WHO) estimates that about 25 percent of the world's population is infected by one or more kinds of parasitic worms.

- The world's deadliest parasite is the one that causes malaria. Scientists estimate that this parasite has caused more than half of all human deaths from infections since the Stone Age.
- The world is home to 3,200 kinds of parasites.
- Giardia is the most prevalent intestinal parasite in humans; it is found in unclean drinking water and causes weakness, stomach bloating, diarrhea, and poor absorption of nutrients.
- The longest tapeworm ever recorded in a person was removed from Sally Mae Wallace of Mississippi in 1991 and measured 37 feet (11.3m) long.

Antimicrobial Drugs

- In 2007 the Centers for Disease Control and Prevention reported that antibiotics were prescribed unnecessarily for the common cold 18 million times despite the fact that antibiotics cannot affect viruses.
- According to WHO, more than half the world's antibiotics are used on farm animals, not people, and this use may be increasing the incidence of drug-resistant bacteria.
- Scientists have developed more than 150 antibiotics against bacterial diseases.
- In developed countries about 60 percent of hospital-acquired infections are from drug-resistant bacteria.
- Four antiviral drugs are FDA approved for treating influenza; although these drugs cannot cure influenza, they can shorten the time of illness by one or two days.
- Current WHO guidelines recommend that HIV infections be treated with a combination of at least three antiretroviral drugs at all times.
- By 2008, according to WHO, more than 4 million people in developing countries were receiving antiretroviral drug treatment for HIV infection.

Vaccines

- As of 2010 the FDA listed 68 vaccines approved for use in the United States.
- When the Global Polio Eradication Initiative began a mass vaccination strategy in 1988, more than 1,000 children worldwide were paralyzed

by polio every day. In 2009 fewer than 2,000 cases were reported in the world for the entire year.

- According to WHO, in 2009 the number of children worldwide dying every year fell below 10 million for the first time in history, due in large part to global vaccination programs.
- In 2009 WHO reported that more than 30 new vaccine preparations for major diseases for which no vaccines exist were "in the pipeline," undergoing human testing and clinical trials and close to being submitted for government or WHO approval.
- The US government's Congressional Budget Office estimates that, on average, to get a new vaccine from the laboratory to the marketplace takes 10 years, and the cost is at least $100 million to complete all the necessary testing in order to apply for FDA approval.

Related Organizations

Bill and Melinda Gates Foundation

PO Box 23350
Seattle, WA 98102
phone: (206) 709-3100
website: www.gatesfoundation.org

The Gates Foundation is a philanthropic organization that has provided major funding for vaccine research and distribution in the developing world. The foundation has pledged $10 billion for new vaccine development, calling it a critical global need for the twenty-first century.

Centers for Disease Control and Prevention (CDC)

1600 Clifton Rd.
Atlanta, GA 30333
phone: (800) 232-4636
website: www.cdc.gov

The CDC provides extensive, up-to-date information about infectious diseases, treatment, and prevention.

Doctors Without Borders (MSF USA)

333 Seventh Ave., 2nd Floor
New York, NY 10001-5004
phone: (212) 679-6800
website: www.doctorswithoutborders.org

Dedicated to providing emergency medical assistance in 70 countries throughout the world, Médecins Sans Frontières (or Doctors Without Borders) is on the leading edge in getting up-to-date medical treatments, vaccines, and rapid, accurate diagnosis to people in the developing world.

Infectious Disease Research Institute

1124 Columbia St., Suite 400
Seattle, WA 98104
phone: (206) 381-0883
website: www.idri.org

This nonprofit organization is dedicated to research involving the diagnosis, treatment, and prevention of infectious diseases of the world's poor. It concentrates on leishmaniasis, Chagas disease, tuberculosis, malaria, and leprosy.

Infectious Diseases Society of America (IDSA)

1300 Wilson Blvd., Suite 300
Arlington, VA 22209
phone: (703) 299-0200
website: www.idsociety.org

IDSA is an organization of scientists, medical professionals, and other health care workers who specialize in infectious diseases. Its mission is to fight for solutions to antimicrobial resistance and to campaign for 10 new antibiotics by 2020.

International AIDS Vaccine Initiative

110 William St., Floor 27
New York, NY 10038-3901
phone: (212) 847-1111
website: www.iavi.org

IAVI's core mission is to support the development of AIDS vaccines through research and assessment of ongoing trials of proposed preventive medicines.

National Foundation for Infectious Diseases (NFID)

4733 Bethesda Ave., Suite 750
Bethesda, MD 20814
phone: (301) 656-0003
website: www.nfid.org

The NFID is a nonprofit organization dedicated to educating the public and health care professionals about the cause, treatment, and prevention of infectious disease.

US Food and Drug Administration (FDA)

10903 New Hampshire Ave.
Silver Spring, MD 20993-0002
phone: (888) 463-6332
website: www.fda.gov

The FDA is the federal government's regulatory agency for evaluating and approving new drugs and vaccines.

For Further Research

Books

Donald Emmeluth, *Plague*. New York: Chelsea House, 2009.

Connie Goldsmith, *Battling Malaria: On the Front Lines Against a Global Killer*. Brookfield, CT: Twenty-First Century, 2010.

Linley Erin Hall, *Killer Viruses*. New York: Rosen Central, 2010.

Debra A. Miller, *Resistant Infections*. Farmington Hills, MI: Greenhaven, 2009.

Tamra Orr, *Polio*. New York: Rosen, 2010.

Kara Rogers, ed., *Infectious Diseases*. New York: Rosen, 2011.

Joaquima Serradell, *SARS*. New York: Chelsea House, 2009.

Stephanie Watson, *Superbugs: The Rise of Drug-Resistant Germs*. New York: Rosen, 2010.

Websites

The Big Picture Book of Viruses (www.virology.net/Big_Virology/BV HomePage.html). At this site from Tulane University, visitors can see electron microscope photographs of different infectious viruses, along with a description of each virus.

Carter Center Guinea Worm Disease Eradication (www.cartercenter. org/health/guinea_worm/mini_site/index.html). The Carter Center maintains a map of guinea worm eradication success, as well as facts and information about the eradication program. Visitors can watch a video of the "Countdown to Zero."

On Being a Scientist: A Guide to Responsible Conduct in Research (www.nap.edu/openbook.php?record_id=12192&page=R1). This is a free, downloadable book from the National Academy of Sciences Committee on Science, Engineering, and Public Policy. The 2009 edition provides a clear explanation of the responsible conduct of scientific research. Chapters on treatment of data, mistakes and negligence, the scientist's role in society, and other topics offer invaluable insight for student researchers.

Parasite Images, Chiang Mai University, Thailand (www.medicine. cmu.ac.th/dept/parasite/image.htm). Enter the site by clicking on one of the types of parasites. (Cestode, for example, includes tapeworms.) See the different stages of the parasite, such as egg, cyst, and adult.

Virtual Museum of Bacteria (www.bacteriamuseum.org). Learn about both beneficial and pathogenic bacteria at this website. It also provides information about the immune system, antibiotics, and vaccines.

World Health Organization (WHO) (www.who.int/en). The WHO website provides up-to-date news about the state of infectious disease problems around the world. Some topics include latest outbreaks, the need for new antibiotics, and the new medicines and vaccines being investigated.

Index

Note: Boldface page numbers indicate illustrations.

Jenner, Edward, 8

Kabayo, John, 56–57
Koch, Robert, 8, 19, 21

larva, definition of, 31
lavender oil, 44
Leeuwenhoek, Antoni van, 8,
    18–19
Legionnaires' disease, 23
leishmaniasis. *See* visceral
    leishmaniasis
leprosy (Hansen's disease),
    58–60, **59**
lesion, definition of, 28
Lister, Joseph, 8, 19
Lyme disease, 23
lymphatic filiariasis
    (elephantiasis), 12

Maalin, Ali Maow, 50
malaria, 40–42
    spread of, **73**
Maraviroc, 43–45
Martin, Joseph A., 43
Mattey, Mike, 48
melarsoprol, 38, 39
MenAfriVac, 9

methicillin-resistant
    Staphylococcus aureus
    (MRSA), 9, 41, 45–47,
    46
    prevention strategies,
        60–61
    use of bacteriophages
        against, 48, 66–68
microbes
    adaptability of, 24, 26
    culture of, 33
    discovery of, 19
    immune system as defense
        against, 21
    See also bacterium/bacteria;
        viruses
Mitano, 59
Montagnier, Luc, 33
MRSA. *See* methicillin-
    resistant *Staphylococcus
    aureus*
mutations, 26
    definition of, 22
    in HIV, 34–35
    in response to antimicrobial
        drug treatment, 49
Mycobacterium tuberculosis,
    28–29

Naegleria fowleri (amoeba), 14,
    15
Nagami, Pamela, 28

National Foundation for Infectious Diseases (NFID), 83

National Institute of Allergy and Infectious Diseases (NIAID), 12–13, 71

Newland, Jason, 46

nifurtimox, 40

orphan diseases, 58

Pan African Tsetse and Trypanosomiasis Eradication Campaign (PATTEC), 56

parasites, 26

Pasteur, Louis, 8, 19–21, **20**

pathogens
classification of, 15–16
definition of, 15

penicillin, 8, 18, 22

Piarroux, Renaud, 11

Pinto, Eugenia, 44

Plasmodium, 41

prevention strategies
for Guinea worm disease, 50–54
for MRSA, 60–61

public health interventions, 60–61

for rheumatic fever, 61–62

for sleeping sickness (HAT), 54–57

vaccines, 57–58
for herpes simplex, 52
for HIV, 70–72
for leprosy, 59–60
for malaria, 72–74
for tuberculosis, 67

Priotto, Gerardo, 38, 39–40

protease inhibitors, definition of, 43

rabies, 21, 23

Raviglione, Mario, 31

Redshaw, Sally, 43

reservoirs, 23

resistance, antibiotic, definition of, 24

rheumatic fever, 61

ribosomes, definition of, 68

RNA (ribonucleic acid), 24
viral, research on drugs targeting, 69

Sachs, Jessica Snyder, 16, 47

Salgueiro, Ligia, 44

Salk, Jonas, 9

Salmonella, 36

Sazawal, Sunmil, 12

viruses, 24
  adaptability of, 26
  process of infection, **25**
visceral leishmaniasis (VL),
  31–32

Wade, Brock, 45–46
Wehrle, Janna, 68
Wherry, John, 70

Wood, Tony, 45
World Health Organization
  (WHO), 10, 31, 42

Yoder, Jonathan, 14

zidovudine (AZT), 43

Picture Credits

Cover: iStockphoto.com

Maury Aaseng: 25

© Jorge Adorno/Reuters/Corbis: 59

AP Images: 11

Scott Camazine/Science Photo Library: 46

Jean-Loup Charmet/Science Photo Library: 20

© Corbis: 17

Thomas Deerinck, NCMIR/Science Photo Library: 71

Martin Dohrn/Science Photo Library: 39

Eye of Science/Photo Researchers, Inc: 29

© Louise Gubb/Corbis: 55

NYPL/Science Source/Science Photo Library: 51

Philppe Psaila/Science Photo Library: 64

Martin M. Rotker/Science Photo Library: 34

Thinkstock/iStockphoto.com: 8 (lower right), 9 (bottom)

Thinkstock/Photodisc: 9 (top)

Thinkstock/Photos.com: 8 (top, lower left)

Steve Zmina: 73

About the Author

Toney Allman holds degrees from Ohio State University and the University of Hawaii. She currently lives in Virginia, where she enjoys a rural lifestyle as well as researching and writing about a variety of topics for students.